# ASTYPALAIA

Thodoris Kiousis

# CONTENTS

# CONTRIBUTORS

**PUBLISHER**
Apostolis Nakas

**RESEARCH – TEXT**
Thodoris Kiousis

**PHOTOGRAPHIC MATERIAL**
Thodoris Kiousis
Vassiliki Hadjiantoniou
Dimitris Giannelos

**EDITOR**
Sofia Politou-Ververi

**DESIGN – LAYOUT**
Pelagia Baka

**STUDIO**
Diana Poikilidou

**GIS MAPPING**
Ioanna-Liana Tolika



**1st Edition, March 2016**

*Member of*
**NAKAS GROUP**

23th km of Marathonos Avenue, Rafina, Attica, Greece 19009, Tel.: +30 22940 79816
info@road.gr • **www.road.gr**

The Blue Star ferry always arrives from Piraeus late at night. After a few dark kilometres from the port of AGIOS Andréas and just before we enter the old port of Péra Gialós, Chóra, with its milky-white little houses glowing on the slope and sliding down to the sea, emerges on the hill. On top of them, the illuminated castle shines like a crown while the full bright moon on the background unfolds its silver path on the Aegean waters that embrace Astypálaia.

This is the fabulous picture I saw before my very eyes when I first visited the island ten years ago. Despite the ten-hour trip and the late time of arrival, I was so much surprised that I stayed admiring it until the daybreak, before I finally fell asleep and in love...

The sunlight in Astypálaia reveals much more than the moonlight indicates! The two wings of the "Aegean butterfly" (as this magical island is often called due to its shape) will fly your senses to the highest levels of carelessness, tranquility and pleasure. You will swim in dozens of sinuous coasts washed by emerald waters and admire pretty little churches and monuments built in many different periods all around the island. Taste fresh fish and pure Greek cuisine, all typical of an island. When you walk along a path it is impossible to resist the fine scent of thyme, while wild rabbits and partridges will definitely throw a glance at you and the view all around will be breathtaking! It is only certain that you will get lost as you wander around the scenic snowy-white little alleys and admire the castle that has been praised in many songs. Have fun in pretty little bars and join the other visitors of the island and the friendly locals. The island has very positive energy!

Tourist infrastructures are of a very good level and meet all the requirements. Comfortable rooms, most of them with a wonderful view, traditional hotels and boutiques, perhaps the best campsite of the Aegean, all of them being in perfect harmony with the traditional architecture and the environment. Easy transportation by municipal bus fleets that run the entire asphalt network and by very reliable cars and motorbikes in car rentals. Homemade food and gourmet dishes in local taverns and restaurants. Lots of cultural events, concerts, live groups, happenings, exhibitions and other events hosted by the municipality, the active cultural association of the island and the owners of amusement places. Short trips to nearby islands and inaccessible beaches. Good market with local products, souvenirs, brands and more sophisticated items. Prices cover a wide range and are more than good...

I hope through this book I can give you the magic energy of Astypálaia and help you become acquainted with all its aspects. In order to better assimilate the information of this guide, you had better get the respective new Best of Astypálaia map from Nakas ROAD Cartography.

Let's go...

***P.S.*** *Warning: It is very possible to fall in love (with Astypálaia)!*

**THODORIS KIOUSIS**

## ACKNOWLEDGEMENTS

*There are many people I would like to thank because they helped me with the publication of this guide:*

*The publishers Giórgos & Apostolis Nákas, who embraced this initiative without any doubts,*

*The deputy mayor Maria Kamboúri for her cooperation and mainly for the photographic material,*

*Ms Stella Papadimitríou for her help with bibliography,*

*Father Efsévios Stavlás for the tour of Portaítissa and other churches of the island,*

*Ms Ioánna Mariáki, president of the Cultural and Educational Association of Astypálaia*

*Ms Eléni Markóni for her traditional recipes and the exciting stories of the Italian period,*

*Mr. Michális Giánnaros and Mr. Dimítris Petrídenas for the traditional products,*

*Ms Mary Bouzalá for all the information about entertainment,*

*Ms Varvára Aggelídi for... everything.*

# GEOGRAPHY

Astypálaia is situated in the south east Aegean. It belongs to the Prefecture of the Dodecanese (the westernmost island) but in geographic and cultural terms it is a bridge between the Dodecanese and the Cyclades. It is surrounded by Amorgós to the NW (23 miles), Kos to the NE (23 miles), Anáfi to the SW (27 miles) and Sýrna to the SE (18 miles), which also belongs to the Dodecanese. The coordinates that form the notional rectangle surrounding Astypálaia are: 36°30.5 and 36°39 N as well as 26°15.5 and 26°28.6 E. It covers an area of 96.42 square km (5th largest island of the Dodecanese) and its coasts are 110 km long (!) The island could be described as a meandering butterfly due to its shape. Its maximum length (from Ármenos Cape to the east to Poúlaris Cape to the west) is 19 km, while its narrowest point, which is called Stenó and connects the two wings of the butterfly, is only 105 m wide and serves as a bridge between Mésa Nisí (inner island) to the east and Éxo Nisí (outer island) to the west. The land is semi-mountainous, with highest points being the summits of Várdia (482 m), Ftéra (447 m) in Éxo Nisí and Kasteládnos (366 m) in Mésa Nisí. The largest level areas are Livádia, with the namesake settlement to the west of Chóra, and the area of Análipsi in the narrow strip of the butterfly. A similar plain also exists at the deepest point of the cove of Vathý in Mésa Nisí. Two remarkable plateaus are formed in the central part of Éxo Nisí, from north to south: Messariá and Armenochóri, respectively. There are no rivers in Astypálaia, only torrents, the main of them being Kakós Potamós (bad river), which is fed in Messariá and falls into the cove of Pachiá 'Ammos to the NW, Soulountránis, which flows down from Várdia to Kaminákia to the S, the torrent of Vátses, which ends at the namesake beach to the S, and the torrent of Livádia. An artificial lake has been created, with the help of an earth dam, in the course of the torrent of Livádia. The lake irrigates the plain and supplies the entire island with water. Astypálaia is surrounded by numerous islets and reefs that belong to the island. The three Fokonísia Islands (Fókia, agios

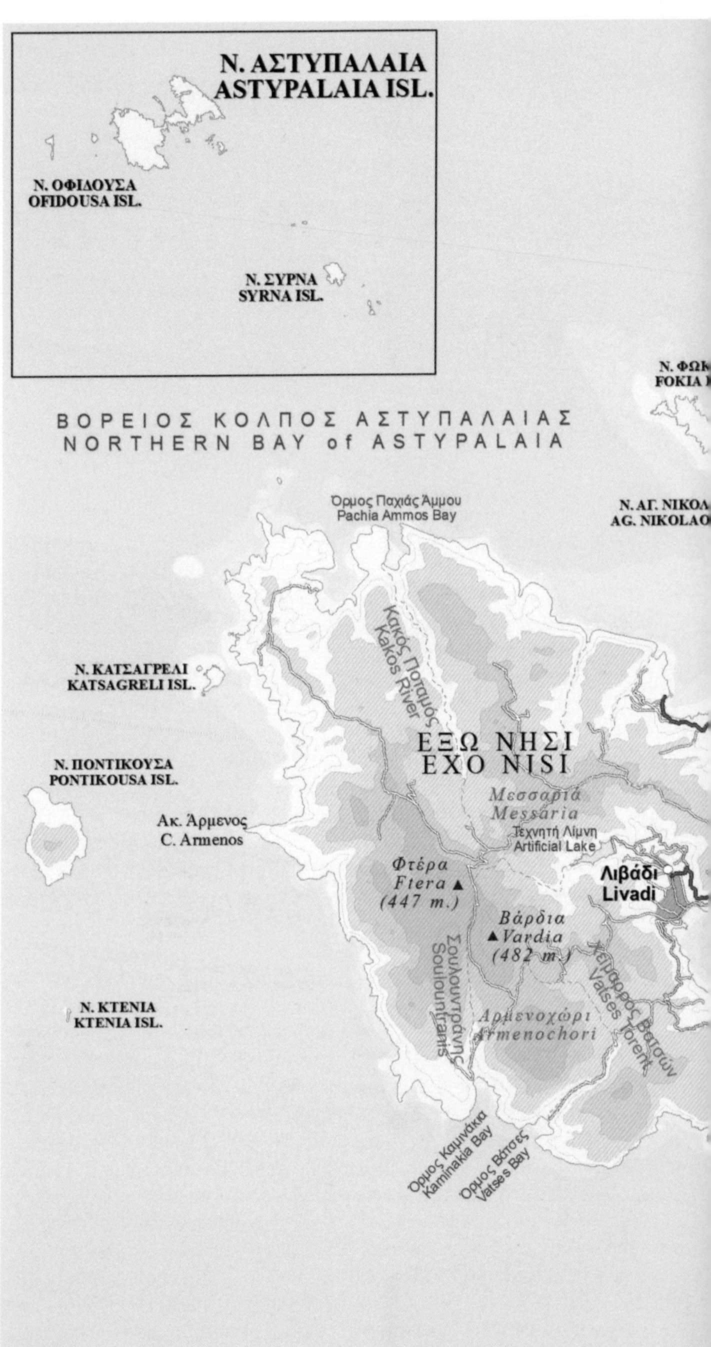
Ν. ΑΣΤΥΠΑΛΑΙΑ
ASTYPALAIA ISL.
Ν. ΟΦΙΔΟΥΣΑ
OFIDOUSA ISL.
Ν. ΣΥΡΝΑ
SYRNA ISL.
ΒΟΡΕΙΟΣ ΚΟΛΠΟΣ ΑΣΤΥΠΑΛΑΙΑΣ
NORTHERN BAY of ASTYPALAIA
Όρμος Παχιάς Άμμου
Pachia Ammos Bay
Ν. ΚΑΤΣΑΓΡΕΛΙ
KATSAGRELI ISL.
Κακός Ποταμός
Kakos River
ΕΞΩ ΝΗΣΙ
EXO NISI
Ν. ΠΟΝΤΙΚΟΥΣΑ
PONTIKOUSA ISL.
Ακ. Άρμενος
C. Armenos
Μεσσαριά
Messaria
Τεχνητή Λίμνη
Artificial Lake
Φτέρα
Ftera
(447 m.)
Λιβάδι
Livadi
Βάρδια
Vardia
(482 m.)
Σουλουντράνης
Soulountranis
Χείμαρρος Βατσών
Valtses Torrent
Ν. ΚΤΕΝΙΑ
KTENIA ISL.
Αρμενοχώρι
Armenochori
Όρμος Καμινάκια
Kaminakia Bay
Όρμος Βάτσες
Vatses Bay

Ν. ΑΣΤΥΠΑΛΑΙΑ
ASTYPALAIA ISL.
Βαθύ
Vathi
ΜΕΣΑ ΝΗΣΙ
MESA NISI
Καστελάνος
Kastelanos
(366 m.)
Ν. ΜΑΞΙΛΑΡΙ
MAXILARI ISL.
Ανάληψη (Μαλτεζάνα)
Analipsi (Maltezana)
Ακ. Πούλαρης
C. Poularis
Στενό
Steno
Ν. ΧΟΝΔΡΟ
HONDRO ISL.
Ν. ΛΙΓΝΟ
LIGNO ISL.
Ν. ΚΟΥΤΣΟΜΥΤΗΣ
KOUTSOMYTIS ISL.
Ν. ΤΗΓΑΝΙ
TIGANI ISL.
Ν. ΑΓ. ΚΥΡΙΑΚΗ
AG. KYRIAKI ISL.
Ν. ΜΟΝΗ
MONI ISL.
Ν. ΦΤΕΝΟ
FTENO ISL.
Ν. ΧΟΝΔΡΟΠΟΥΛΟ
HONDROPOULO ISL.
Ν. ΚΟΥΝΟΥΠΟΙ
KOUNOUPOI ISL.
ΝΟΤΙΟΣ ΚΟΛΠΟΣ ΑΣΤΥΠΑΛΑΙΑΣ
SOUTHERN BAY of ASTYPALAIA

Nikólaos and Maxilári) are situated at the centre of the northern bay. To the west, from the nearest to the remotest, are the islets of Katsagréli, Pontikoúsa, Kténia and Ofidoúsa. In the southern bay, opposite Maltezána, are the islets of Hondró, Lignó and AGIOS Kyriakí, while a little farther, to the SE, Koutsomýtis, Tigáni, Moní, Ftenó, Hondrópoulo and Kounoúpoi with its marvellous beach. The remotest of all is Sýrna, 18 miles to the SE, which also has its own cluster of islets (Adelfés, Sofrána, Karavonísia, Tría Nisiá, etc.).

Astypálaia belongs to the district of Kálymnos of the Prefecture of the Dodecanese (Prefecture of South Aegean) and, along with all the nearby islands, forms a single municipality. According to the 2011 census, the population is 1,334. The village of Chóra (pop. 1,055) is the capital; other villages are Análipsi (pop. 155), Livádi or Maltezána (pop. 110) and Vathý (pop. 14).

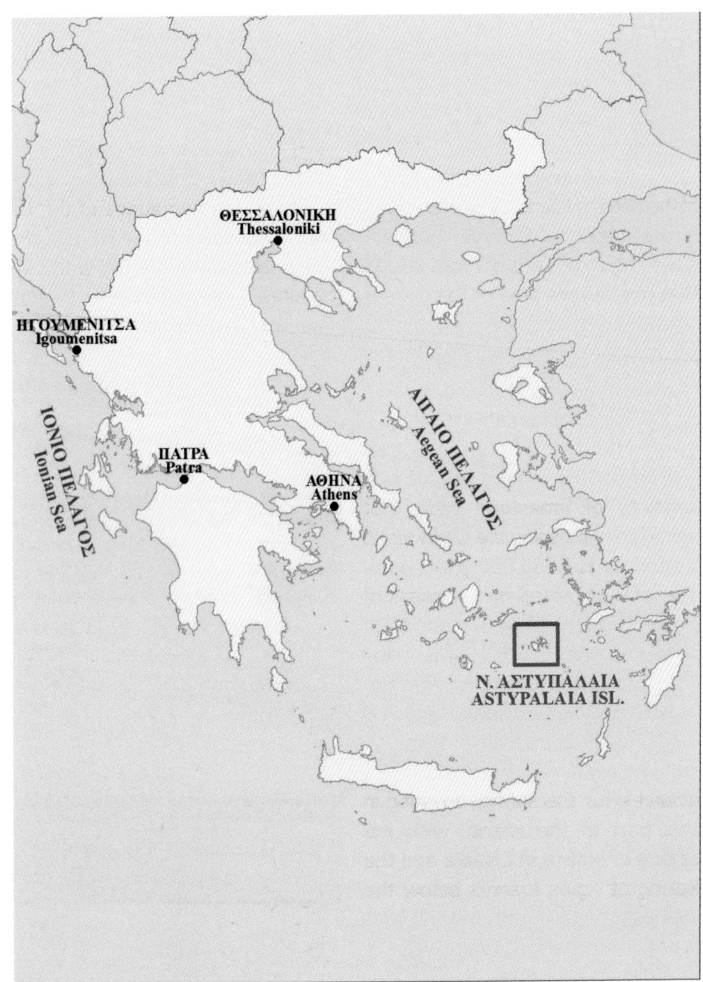

# GEOLOGY

The geological history of Astypálaia is almost identical to that of the rest of the Aegean Islands. The island was formed after successive submersions and emersions of Aigiís (a land that covered the area of the current archipelago millions of years ago).

The three parts of the island have slightly different geological identities with regard to their composition and the geological period their beds of rocks were formed: Mésa Nisí consists of limestone beds that were formed during the Cretaceous Period (c. 100,000,000 years ago). The interior central part consists of flysch and the coasts consist of porous stone. Éxo Nisí was made from limestone of the Eocene Period (c. 50.000.000 years ago) and flysch, which is "responsible" (due to its ability to contain water resources) for the springs existing in this part of the island, with the spring of Mourá in Livádia and the spring of Agios Ioánnis below the namesake mona-stery to the west being the most important.

The limestone has "donated" to Astypálaia two caves of exceptional beauty on the two edges of the island: Drakospiliá to the NE and the cave of Négrou to the SW with stalagmites and stalactites, though none of them has been developed.

**The 1956 earthquake**

At dawn of July 9, 1956, a mighty earthquake 7.5 R, whose epicenter was in the submarine area between Amorgós and Astypálaia, shook the small island to its foundations! The size of the earthquake caused a tsunami 25 m high that struck the coasts of Astypálaia at a speed of 300 km per hour. It was then that many houses inside the castle collapsed.

In Livádi, shortly before the powerful wave struck, the sea water –which had turned from blue to grey– receded 100 m from the seashore and when it returned, it advanced 400 m into the plain and flooded it.

There was extensive damage to the port of Péra Gialós, where all fishing boats were destroyed.

It was the greatest tsunami ever been recorded in the Aegean!

# FLORA & FAUNA

The first picture the visitor sees is that of a Cycladic island without trees and vegetation rather than an island of the Dodecanese. But this is not the case! Most of plant species native to the Aegean grow in Astypálaia: chamomile, Aegean arenaria, chromophytes, blue-bells, wild carnations. There are rare and protected plants, such as: birthwort, wild cumin, scammony, flax, etc. The vegetation in the east part of the island is described by juniper shrub, pistacia and scant brushwood. The biodiversity is evident in the east part of the island (Mésa Nisí) and the nearby islets, which are included in Natura 2000 environmental network. The west part has mainly brushwood (thorny burnet, etc.), while the torrent beds are full of osiers, oleanders and fig trees. In coastal settlements, mainly in Livádia, to the south of the dam, the visitor can see olives, figs and tamarisks as well as conifer trees, reeds and vineyards. The pres-

Wild saffron grows on the north slopes of Éxo Nisí

Aegean cats taking a siesta in an alley of Chóra

ence of aromatic-pharmaceutical herbs is identified with the landscape of Astypálaia and the visitors to the island are overwhelmed by the strong smells of native vegetation (thyme, oregano and sage). The wild and rare saffron (zaforá, according to the locals) grows to the north of Éxo Nisí and is collected every November. The stamens of saffron flowers are widely used in local cuisine and confectionery.

The complete absence of snakes is a typical feature of the local fauna, a fact already known from antiquity: "...the land of Astypálaia is a great enemy of snakes," Aristotle says. As for other species, there are high numbers of small rodents, hares and wild rabbits, although the island is a destination for hunters who arrive from all nearby islands.

There is also a rich variety of birds: Cory's shearwaters, Eleonora's falcons and shags nest mainly in the small islets, while silver gulls, Aegean gulls as well as partridges and red-backed shrikes find shelter in the mountains.

However, the dominant species on the island is the Aegean cat (recently officially recognized species), the trademark of Astypálaia and generally all Aegean Islands! The land of Ichthyóessa, as the island was called by the Romans (from the ancient Greek word ichthýs meaning fish), has also a rich marine life. The seabed is full of extensive areas with posidonia, an aquatic plant forming underwater meadows that enrich the water with oxygen.

As a result, the bottom and the waters of Astypálaia are full of life! The sea caves and the nearby islands provide refuge to the Mediterranean monk seal monachus monachus, while bottlenose dolphins, striped dolphins, green turtles and sea turtles caretta caretta appear at times.

The overpopulation of hares in ancient years was such a serious problem for the locals that the City sent a delegation to the Delphi Oracle to ask for advice.

The historian Igísandros reports Pythía's answer: "Breed dogs from Lakonía (Sparta) and go hunting." Indeed, the people of Astypálaia brought hunting dogs from Sparta (they were considered the best in ancient Greece) and they soon got rid of the hares!

# GETTING THERE

## Passenger Ships

Astypálaia has 2 ports. The old port of Péra Gialós or Skála below Chóra serves local connection with Kálymnos (29 miles) 3 times a week (trip takes 3.5 hours).

The second port is to the NE of Éxo Nisí, in the cove of Agios Andréas, within 6 km from Chóra. It was originally built (late 2003) as an alternative solution whenever the strong south winds are blowing in Péra Gialós, before it was chosen to be the main port that serves the connection with Piraeus (two ferry lines-117 miles), the Cyclades and the Dodecanese. There is a small waiting room and a bar.

The trip from Piraeus takes approximately 10 hours and there are 3 to 5 trips a week, depending on the ship and the season.As for the first line, Astypálaia is the last port of the ship after the Cyclades (Sýros, Páros, Náxos, Amorgós and Donoúsa), while it is the first port the ship stops at in the second line (once a week), when the ship sails to the Dodecanese (Kálymnos, Kos, Nísyros, Tílos and Rhodes). All ships serving Astypálaia can carry cars as well.

The port of Agios Andréas

## Airplane

The airport (IATA code: JTY) is situated on a plateau in the area of Análipsi, within 10 km from Chóra.

Six flights (duration 1 hour) a week (4 in winter), using small aircraft of Olympic Air/Aegean, connect Astypálaia with Athens International Airport "Eleftherios Venizelos".

The same airliner connects the island 3 times a week (2 in winter) with Rhodes, Kos, Kálymnos and Léros.

It is important to know that the national airport of Astypálaia also includes military facilities so photographs are prohibited in the area!

The building of the "Astypálaia Island National Airport" (JTY)

## Private Vessel

In the old port of Péra Gialós there is a new marina for vessels, equipped with water and electricity supply. Fuel is easily supplied with the help of road tankers belonging to the two petrol stations of the island. Communication with the port is through Channel 12 in VHF and Channel 23 in Olympia radio.

The toll for the ship is very reasonable, while customs services are accommodated in the building of port authorities in Péra Gialós. You can get your supplies from the mini market of Vogiatzís (0030 22430 61247), a few metres from the marina as well as from other shops of the island.

Private vessels in the new marina of the port of Péra Gialós

## Travel Agencies

**PARADISE TRAVEL:**
Péra Gialós,
Tel. : (0030) 2243061224,
Fax: (0030) 2243061450,
paradisostravel@yahoo.gr
*(central agency of Blue Star Ferries)*

**ELEMENTI TRAVEL**
General Travel Agency:
Péra Gialós,
Tel.: (0030) 2243059868,
Fax: (0030) 2243062130,
vogiatzis_ros_s@yahoo.com
www.astypalea-travel.com

**ASTYPALEA TOURS:**
Péra Gialós,
Tel.: (0030) 2243061571-2,
Fax: (0030) 2243061328,
Mobile: (0030) 6945431485
ja@astypaleatours.gr,
www.astypaleatours.gr
*(Olympic Air/Aegean, central agency of ANEK - Anonymous Ferry Company Municipality of Kalymnos)*

# GETTING AROUND

## Bus

For those who want to get around the island, the Municipality, in cooperation with a local citizen who owns the second ferry line, runs two bus lines that serve almost the entire asphalt road network of the island.

The ticket is very reasonable and the buses are quite frequent. There is also Elementi Bus of the namesake agency, which organizes daily trips to the remote beaches of the island: Tzanáki, Agios Konstantínos, Vátses and Kaminákia.

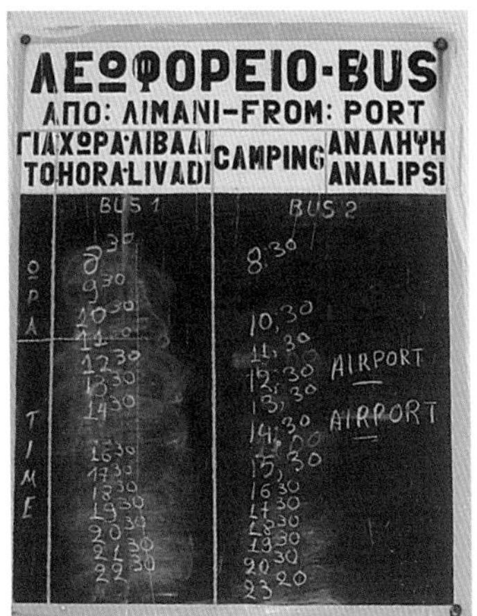

**LINE 1: PORT – TZANÁKI**
Port, Péra Gialós, Iatreío, Anemómyloi, Pigádi, Livádi Beach, AGIOS Vassíleios, Tzanáki Beach.

**LINE 2: PORT – SCHINÓNTAS**
Port, Péra Gialós, Campsite, Marmári, Agios Andréas (when ship arrives) Port, Stenó, Plákes Beach, Airport (when aircraft arrives), Maltezána, Schinóntas

# DISTANCES

| | CHORA | LIVADI | ANALIPSI | MESA VATHY | PORT AG. ANDREAS | AIRPORT | KAMINAKIA |
|---|---|---|---|---|---|---|---|
| CHORA | X | 1 | 10 | 22 | 6 | 10 | 10 |
| LIVADI | 1 | X | 11 | 23 | 7 | 11 | 9 |
| ANALIPSI | 10 | 11 | X | 12 | 6 | 1 | 20 |
| MESA VATHY | 22 | 23 | 12 | X | 18 | 13 | 32 |
| PORT AG. ANDREAS | 6 | 7 | 6 | 13 | X | 7 | 16 |
| AIRPORT | 10 | 11 | 1 | 13 | 7 | X | 20 |
| KAMINAKIA | 10 | 9 | 20 | 32 | 16 | 20 | X |
| VATSES | 7 | 6 | 17 | 29 | 13 | 17 | 9 |
| AGIOS IOANNIS | 11 | 12 | 21 | 33 | 17 | 21 | 7 |
| PANORMOS | 14 | 15 | 24 | 36 | 20 | 24 | 12 |
| FLEVARIOTISSA | 6 | 7 | 16 | 28 | 12 | 16 | 8 |
| AGIOS KONSTANTINOS | 5 | 4 | 15 | 27 | 11 | 15 | 8 |
| AGRELIDI | 16 | 17 | 6 | 6 | 12 | 7 | 26 |
| PANAGIA POULARIANI | 20 | 21 | 10 | 8 | 16 | 11 | 30 |
| CAMPSITE | 4 | 5 | 6 | 18 | 3 | 6 | 14 |
| STENO | 7 | 8 | 3 | 15 | 3 | 3 | 17 |

# IN KILOMETRE

| VATSES | AGIOS IOANNIS | PANORMOS | FLEVARIOTISSA | AGIOS KONSTANTINOS | AGRELIDI | PANAGIA POULARIANI | CAMPSITE | STENO |
|---|---|---|---|---|---|---|---|---|
| 7 | 11 | 14 | 6 | 5 | 16 | 20 | 4 | 7 |
| 6 | 12 | 15 | 7 | 4 | 17 | 21 | 5 | 8 |
| 17 | 21 | 24 | 16 | 15 | 6 | 10 | 6 | 3 |
| 29 | 33 | 36 | 28 | 27 | 6 | 8 | 18 | 15 |
| 13 | 17 | 20 | 12 | 11 | 12 | 16 | 3 | 3 |
| 17 | 21 | 24 | 16 | 15 | 7 | 11 | 6 | 3 |
| 9 | 7 | 12 | 8 | 8 | 26 | 30 | 14 | 17 |
| X | 14 | 19 | 13 | 6 | 23 | 27 | 11 | 14 |
| 14 | X | 7 | 7 | 13 | 27 | 31 | 15 | 18 |
| 19 | 7 | X | 12 | 19 | 30 | 34 | 18 | 21 |
| 13 | 7 | 12 | X | 11 | 22 | 26 | 10 | 13 |
| 6 | 13 | 19 | 11 | X | 21 | 25 | 9 | 12 |
| 23 | 27 | 30 | 22 | 21 | X | 6 | 12 | 9 |
| 27 | 31 | 34 | 26 | 25 | 6 | X | 16 | 13 |
| 11 | 15 | 18 | 10 | 9 | 12 | 16 | X | 3 |
| 14 | 18 | 21 | 13 | 12 | 9 | 13 | 3 | X |

** The red routes are via Várdia – Stavrós*

## Taxi

On the island there are two taxis:
**1)** Giorgos-Pantelis: (0030) 6976256461 **2)** Kiki Kali (0030) 6975706365

## Car Rentals

A very good fleet of cars, motorbikes and scooters is available at the four car rentals.

**VERGOULI MOTO / CAR RENTALS.**
Pera Gialos,
**Tel.:** 2243061351,
**Fax:** 2243061765,
**Mob.:** 6970101410,
vergoulisrental@gmail.com,
www.rent-a-car-astypalaia.com

**KYRRANOS RENTALS.**
1o Marmari, **Tel.:** 2243061289,
**Mob.:** 6973546118,
gazozas@hotmail.com

**AGGELIDIS RENT A CAR.**
Pera Gialos, **Tel.:** 2243061087,
**Mob.:** 6976652484,
info@astypalea-rentacar.gr,
www.astypalea-rentacar.gr

**ASTYCAR.**
Pera Gialos, **Tel.:** 2243061263,
astycar@otenet.gr, www.astycar.gr

## Trips

In case you want to visit the nearby islands and the inaccessible beaches of the island, there are 3 vessels that can take you to the islets of Koutsomýti and Kounoúpa, the beaches of Vátses and Kaminákia as well as to Aï-Giánnis to the west in order to admire the wonderful sunset.

Departures are at 10-11 in the morning and the return at 5-6 in the afternoon. You can also hire a vessel after contacting the agency.

**THALASSOPOÚLI.**
Pera Gialos Tel. No.: 6974436338
**NO STRESS MAGGANAS.**
Pera Gialos Tel. No.: 6971754127
**PLOUMI SEA CRUISES.**
Pera Gialos Tel. No.: 6945965158

The "thalassopoúli" (sea bird) will take you to nearby islands and inaccessible beaches

# HISTORY

## Mythology

Astypálaia was the second daughter of Foínikas –son of Agínoras, the king of Foiníki (Phoenicia), and Perimídi [also reported as Agamídi, daughter of King Avgeías of Ílis, and sister of Evrópi (Europe)].

The mythical adventure of her famous sister outshone the beautiful Astypálaia. However, she was so beautiful that a serious conflict was caused between Poseidon and Zeus, the father of gods.

Poseidon stole her –just like Zeus had done with Evrópi– and brought her to the island, which was named after her. Astypálaia was romantically involved with the god of the sea and gave birth to two sons: Evrýpalos, who became king of Kos, and Agkaíos, who reigned in Sámos and became one of the Argonauts.

Map of Stampalia of 1597

The symbolisms and imagination of the Greek Mythology is once again amazing: the ancients want to indicate the origin of the people of the island as well as the influences and the identity of Astypálaia.

## The Name of the Island

The island has been called Astypálaia (there are also some corrupted forms, such as Astropaliá and Astypaliá) for thousands of years. The name is derived from the words Ásty (meaning city) and Palaiá (meaning old).

According to the Byzantine author Stéfanos Vyzántios, the Phoenicians called the island Pýrra due to the reddish colour of its soil (from pyr meaning fire). Other names were Pylaía due to the big number of coves or "gates" (from pýli meaning gate), Theón Trápeza (meaning gods' bank) due to the variety of its products, while the Romans called the island Ichthyóessa due to the abundance of fish in nearby waters (from ichthýs meaning fish).

The Venetians called it Stampália, just like their Italian descendants, centuries later, during the 30-year occupation of the Dodecanese. Several opinions have been recorded on the derivation and origin of the island's name.

It has been said that it could be of Phoenician, Semitic or even Sumerian origin! However, they seem to be ungrounded.

The name of Astypálaia is as manifestly Greek like the island itself.

## Prehistoric - Neolithic Periods, Copper Age (3500-1000 BC)

Excavation finds indicate that Astypálaia was already inhabited in 3500 BC. The Carians (a pre-Hellenic tribe of SW Asia Minor) are said to have been the first settlers. Impressive rock paintings depicting ships have been found in the cove of Vathý. Daggers dating to the Early Cycladic period have also been found.

The island must have been an active part of the so-called Cycladic Civilization, which appeared in the Early Copper Age, in the 3rd millennium BC. This is evidenced by a violin-shaped figurine, typical of that period, and the remains of an Early Cycladic acropolis, which have been found at Vathý, as well as by some amphorae found at Vái and Agios Ioánnis.After 2300 BC all Aegean Islands were thrown into turmoil.

Some settlements are abandoned, others are fortified, burial customs change and commercial interactions become fewer, while new architectural and pottery styles appear, interpreted by some scholars as indications of the arrival of new populations. Indeed, according to Thucydides and Ovid, in the latter's poem "Transfigurations," circa 1800 BC the fleet of King Minos from Crete chases off the Carians and colonizes the island with Minoans.

However, with the exception of some shell-like items found in the island of Sýrna and some indications of a settlement in Vathý, there are no other remarkable finds from the Minoan period. Some 200 years later, after the catastrophic eruption of the Santorini volcano (1650 BC) –which was probably the reason why the Minoan Civilization and its dominance in the Aegean suddenly vanished– the island came under the powerful Achaeans-Mycenaeans, as it happened with the entire Greek land, although there are no historical references or evidence apart from some

Rock painting at Vathý

remarkable burial offerings and the vaulted tombs at Armenochóri, Patélla and Sýgkairos. This must have been the period of the famous Trojan War!

## Geometric and Archaic Periods (1000-500 BC)

Fully identified with all the periods of the Greek history, Astypálaia was occupied by the Dorians, who came from Epidaurus and Troezen of the Peloponnese and Mégara of Attica and colonized the island.

They settled on the site of modern Chóra and probably fortified the area of the castle. Inscriptions in Greek-Dorian language have been found.

According to their customs, the Dorians united their colonies in the form of a confederation, with the sanctuary of one of the colonies being the reference point of the union.

Astypálaia belonged to the Dorian Exápolis (six cities) of Knídos (Cnidus), an ancient Greek city of Asia Minor, at the tip of the peninsula between Kos and Nísyros.

Trópeios Apollo and Poseidon were the gods worshipped by the unofficial Dorian confederation. Astypálaia must have prospered in that period.

The Dorian settlers-inhabitants established their own colony in turn, called Roíteion or Pólion, in the strait of the Hellespont, as reported by the great historian and geographer Strabo. The finds of the globally unique infant cemetery that was disco-

### The Tyrant Phálaris of Astypálaia

*Phálaris is watching the "murderous trial" of the structure he ordered to Perílaos*

The notorious Phálaris, son of Leodámas, came from Astypálaia, which had banished him from the island (when ancient Greeks considered someone dangerous for the city, they usually met once a year, wrote his name on a pottery shard, and when the shards with his name amounted to a specific number, the citizen had to leave the city) for an unknown reason. However, if the rest of his life is taken into account, there must have been a good reason for his banishment! He sought refuge in Acragas (Agrigento) of Sicily, which was also a Dorian colony.

He cunningly took over power (570 - 554 BC) and ruled as a cruel tyrant. In ancient years his name became a byword for cruelty ("phalarism"). The renowned poet Pindar reports that Phálaris once asked from the sculptor Perílaos to construct a hollow bronze ox. When the sculptor delivered his work, the tyrant locked Perílaos inside the ox, lit a fire underneath and started listening to the screams of the sculptor who was burning inside the ox and was moaning like a real ox. The bronze ox was made in such a way that any sound produced inside sounded like a moan. This was one of the ways the warped mind of Phálaris had invented when he wanted to punish someone...

vered at Kylíndra, on the SW slope of the hill of Chóra, are dated mainly to that period (as well as in the following years until the Hellenistic period).

## Classical Period (500-336 BC)

Astypálaia continued thriving in the classical years of the ancient Greek history. According to ancient Greek historians and inscriptions that have been found, the island had an agora, a prytaneíon (seat of the government), a theatre and several temples and sanctuaries dedicated to Poseidon, Artemis, Zeus and Athena, as well as a temple of Eileíthyia (goddess of the pains of birth).

The position and the fate of the island in the Greco-Persian Wars are not known. However, it is certain that, after the wars had finished, between 454 and 424 BC it was a member of the Delian League (as it happened with almost all Aegean Islands) and chose to pay the alliance a tribute of 200 drachmae instead of contributing troops.

Astypálaia became a democratic island and participated in the "Carian tax" [The territory of the alliance was divided into districts. Astypálaia belonged to the respective Carian District or Fóros (tax), which included the Dorian SW Asia Minor and the south Dodecanese].

The object of the alliance was the protection from both the Persians and the future Greek revenge. However, the allies gradually came under the Athenian rule and turned against all other Greek cities-states. The conflict generated the Peloponnesian War, in which Asty-pálaia is not reported to have had any significant involvement.

## Hellenistic Period (336-146 BC)

Perhaps the most glorious period in the history of Astypálaia! The fleet takes part in the campaign of Alexander the Great in a very honorary position as Onesicritus of Astypálaia is the captain of the royal flagship of the Greek emperor! Onesicritus (375-300 BC), who was also a cynical philosopher and student of the famous Diogenes (whom Alexander admired and

### Olympic Champion Kleomídis

A great boxer with immense physical strength. Astypálaia was always proud of him in the athletic games of ancient Greece he participated in. He became a boxing Olympic champion at the 71st Olympic Games in 496 BC, when he defeated his opponent Íkkos of Epidaurus. However, after the match Íkkos yielded to his injuries and died due to the heavy blows he had suffered. The judges stripped Kleomídis of his victory and imposed a fine of 40 talents (a huge amount for that period) on him and his city! The proud Kleomídis returned disappointed to Astypálaia, where he was scorned and ridiculed by his fellow citizens. His deranged state of mind made him one day to break down a pillar that supported the roof of the gymnasium; 60 young men were crushed. After this tragic incident he sought refuge at the sanctuary of Athena, where he locked himself inside a box. When his fellow citizens opened the box, they found nothing inside. According to Pausanias the Traveller, when they asked for an oracle from Delphi, they took the following answer: "Kleomídis of Astypálaia is the last hero and should be honoured as an immortal!"

perhaps that was the reason why Onesicritus was appointed to this prominent position), led the Greek fleet under the commands of Admiral Néarchos from the mouth of the Euphrates to the Indian Sea. He wrote the historical works "How Alexander was educated" and "About Indian peoples."

After Alexander the Great died, Astypálaia was included in the Hellenistic kingdom of the Ptolemies-Lagids of Egypt and prospered. It became a commercial hub in the Aegean due to its safe ports, which provided anchorage and shelter to the Ptolemaic fleet.

The island was so rich at the time that it minted its own coins, while it attracted new settlers from Egypt, Syria and Phrygia of Asia Minor, who established associations and sanctuaries to honour their gods.

## Roman Period (146 BC-330 AD)

The special friendship between the island of Astypálaia and Italy has its roots in this distant period! After the Romans prevailed in ancient Greece, they maintained the commercial and cosmopolitan character of the island and made it a major station in the battle against piracy. In 149 BC they co-signed with Astypálaia two copies of a treaty, which were submitted to the sanctuary of Zeus in the Capitol of Rome and to the sanctuary of Athena on the island. A short excerpt: "For the municipality of the Romans and the municipality of Astypálaia there will be peace and friendship and alliance on land and at sea, and there will never be a war." The treaty was enriched in 105 BC. The Roman Consul Publius Rutillious Rufus and Rodoklís of Astypálaia, son of Antímachos, bring the new copies of the treaty to both cities while Astypálaia is granted the title of CIVITAS FOEDERATA, which is conferred to a confederate autonomous city of the empire with full privileges. Roman colonists settle in Astypálaia and build temples and other public buildings. A number of Roman emperors renew the treaty until the reign of Marcus Antonius Gordianus in 244 AD. Astypálaia honoured the treaty by providing protection to the Roman fleet and pursuing the Aegean pirates.

A 105 BC inscription reports that Ephesus of Asia Minor was raided by pirates, who plundered the coasts and took captives. The people of Astypálaia, following the instructions they had, attacked the pirates without fear, pursued them and freed the Ephesians who were intended to become slaves.

Inscription of the Roman period (museum entrance)

## Byzantine Period (330-1207 AD)

Perhaps the poorest period with regard to historical events and available information! The racial and cultural affinity between Greeks and Romans gave the east part of the empire the opportunity to be fully Hellenized, though it maintained the name and the customs of Rome.

The Roman Empire evolves into the Byzantine Empire, the capital is transferred to Constantinople and the state becomes even more powerful! For many centuries to come, the Aegean will be a peaceful and safe sea, without conflicts between nations. This is also helped by the propagation of Christianity in all the islands as well as in the entire East Roman Empire.

There is no exact information as to when Astypálaia adopted Christianity but, according to evidence from other Aegean islands, it must have happened in the years of Emperor Theodosius I (4th c. AC, probably earlier). Several basilicas (Christian churches in Byzantine style) have adorned Astypálaia since then: the basilica at Karékli is dated back to the late 5th c.

The only thing the historians of that period say about the island is its administrative status: "Province of Islands" until the 6th c. and "Aegean Theme" in subsequent periods. As reported in the treatise Taktiká of Emperor Constantine Porphyrogenitus, the island becomes a bishopric from the 9th c. onwards.

The castle at Aï-Giánnis was built in that period to protect the people from the raids of the Arabs, who appeared in the Aegean and in the foreground of history.

The Arab traveller and geographer Edrisi, who was sent to the Aegean Islands by the Norman king of Sicily Roger II in the mid-12th c., reports that: "Stampalia is well inhabited and rich in oxen and sheep...".

The Early Christian basilica of Agios Vassíleios with the exquisite mosaic floor

View of the castle walls

## Frankish Period (1207- 1537)

After almost a thousand years, the Orthodox Byzantine Empire starts to decline and finally surrenders to the Catholic Frank Crusaders, who deviate from the aim of the fourth Crusade, which was the liberation of the Holy Land, and capture Constantinople on April 13, 1204. The entire Helladic territory is cut up in several small kingdoms, which are divided among the nobles participating in the crusade.

The islands come under the domination of the Doge Enrico Dandolo of the Most Serene Republic of Venice. He in turn decides to distribute them among individual noblemen, who would take over the administrative organization of the islands on condition that Venice would be the dominant power.

The doge's nephew, Marko I Sanudo, successively captures all the Cyclades and Astypálaia, while in 1207 he establishes the Duchy of Archipelago with Náxos as its capital. Astypálaia is ceded to his right-hand man, Count Giovanni I Querini Stampalia. The medieval social and economic system of feudalism of West Europe is now implemented here as well. The notorious castle of the island, the gem of Astypálaia, is built in that period.

After Constantinople was captured by the Franks, the Byzantines were restricted to several small states, such as the Despotate of Epirus, the Empire of Níkaia and the Despotate of Mystrás. However, Emperor Andrónikos Palaiológos takes the initiative and the Byzantine fleet under admiral Likários frees several Aegean islands for 30 years, including Astypálaia, and chases the Venetians away. In 1310, Giovanni III Querini recaptures the island. In 1341, the Turk Emir of Aydin, Omar Morbassan, leader of pirates and adventurers of the time, raids the island and destroys it to its foundations, while the locals that survive and are not captured as slaves abandon the island! The Turks appear in the area and their name becomes a byword for pillage and desolation.

Astypálaia remains deserted and uninhabited for 70 years! On March 30, 1413, Giovanni IV Querini, governor of Tínos and Mýkonos, sends settlers from the two islands to Astypálaia and proclaims himself "Count of Astynéa." The information is also provided by a marble Latin inscription attached on a wall of the castle. The war between Venice and Turkey breaks out in 1536 and proved to be fateful for the domination of the Venetians in the Aegean.

## Turkish Occupation (1537-1912)

In 1537, Sultan Suleiman the Magnificent sends the much feared pirate Hayreddin Barbarossa in charge of the Ottoman fleet to capture all the Aegean Islands that were under Venetian occupation.

**The House of QUERINI**

One of the most powerful families of Venice. They claimed to be descended from the Roman Emperor Galba and contributed to the establishment of the Most Serene Republic of Venice. Until the 17th c. their coat of arms included the Byzantine double-headed eagle. Although the period of their occupation is questioned as for their authoritarian leadership, legends and folk traditions describe them even as saints! Today the visitor of Venice can visit the Querini di Stampalia museum-foundation! They ruled for over 300 years, though with some interruptions:

- **Giovanni I: 1207-1231**
- **Giacomo: 1231-1250**
- **Giovanni II: 1250-1262**
- **Nikolo I: 1262-1269**
- **Giovanni III: 1310-1315**
- **Fantin: 1315-1341**
- **Giovanni IV: 1413-1423**
- **Francesco I: 1423-1462**
- **Nikolo II: 1462-1484**
- **Zuanne: 1484-1523**
- **Francesco II: 1523-1537**

*The Querrini coat of arms*

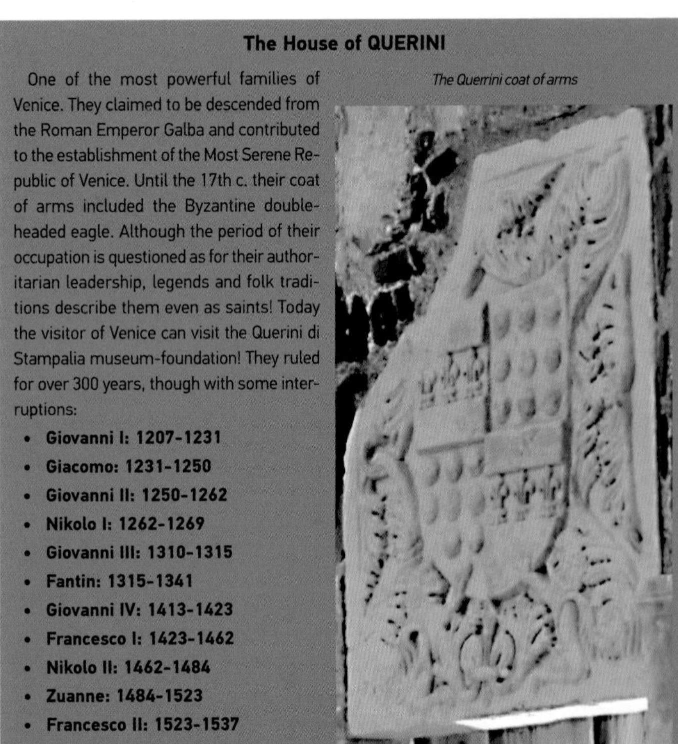

The people of Astypálaia do not hesitate to submit and take advantage of the sultan's pardon and the granting of privileges, as the Ottoman tradition dictated in such cases. The privilege is that the island can be self-governed by its inhabitants (the famous group of Dimogerontía) on only condition that it will pay the Sublime Porte the "maktu" tax.The tax was paid until 1579 to the personal friend of the sultan and Jew banker Josef Nazí, who at first replaced only the title and the duties of the Venetian Duke of Náxos...

Turk officials did not settle in Astypálaia, mainly for the fear of pirates, who every now and then raided all Aegean Islands. Piracy in the Aegean in late medieval years is an everyday matter! The locals get used to living with it and protect their islands and properties, while they in turn become pirates and terrify other areas!

Astypálaia is a typical example. During the Venetian-Turkish war of 1645 – 1669 the locals join the crews of both the Ottoman fleet and the piratical ships that cooperate with the Venetians.

This happens because the island is Ottoman territory and a piratical refuge at the same moment! In any case, after the late 17th c., piracy seems to decline and a period of peace and population growth follows. This information is provided by a number of Greek and European travellers who wrote their impressions from the Aegean Islands.

The 1821 Greek War of Independence finds Astypálaia on the side of the Greek rebels. Dimítrios Thémelis from Pátmos organizes the nearby islands and in the early 1822 the flag of the revolted Greeks is raised in the castle of Astypálaia! Even though the Egyptian allies of the Turks destroyed Kásos, which had the largest and fittest fleet of all the islands of the cluster, the locals were not discouraged but continued fighting at full strength.

Their ships and troops participated in the greatest naval battle of the war, the victorious Naval Battle of Gérontas (opposite Léros), on August 29, 1824, against the united Muslim fleet of Turks, Egyptians, Tunisians and Algerians.

After the 1828 sea battle of Navaríno and the limited independence part of Greece won, the Greek Governor Ioánnis Kapodístrias incorporated Astypálaia in the newly established Greek State.

However, during the 1830 London Conference, when the Greek independence was finalized and modern Greece was officially established, the great European powers decided that the Greek territory would end at the island of Amorgós and Astypálaia would return under the domination of the sultan.

The people were extremely disappointed! The successive letters of protest to the European governments and all relevant authorities that could change the original decision were left unrewarding. After 1870 the Turks revoked the privileges the island had enjoyed for centuries and, as a result, Astypálaia started paying heavy taxes, which in turn led the people to migrate!

The population of the island, which amounts to 4,000 (lots of people had arrived from Kásos after their island had been destroyed by the Egyptians in 1822 and had settled in Astypálaia as refugees), starts decreasing and the locals leave Greece and emigrate to the Greek mainland, USA and Australia.

The sea battle of Gérontas, Giannis Nikou
Source: http://www.iannisnikou.gr

## Italian Occupation and Liberation (1912-1947)

The Ottoman Empire and Italy were involved in a war over Libya in 1911. On April 23, 1912, the Italian fleet under Admiral Presbitero attempted a diversion and captured the Dodecanese starting from Astypálaia.

Italy was supposed to return the Dodecanese to the Turks as soon as the latter walked out of Libya, but the Balkan War that broke out at the moment and the Great War that followed immediately, consolidated the Italian occupation. Almost the same happened in 1918, when Greece started negotiations with Italy in order to annex the Dodecanese.

This time it was the Asia Minor campaign and the subsequent catastrophe of the Greek army as well as the Greek-Turkish war of 1919-1922 that cancelled the plan. On August 6, 1923, Italy officially annexed the Dodecanese to its territory as a possession of the Italian Parliament in the name of King Victor Emmanuelle.

At first, the relationships between the inhabitants and the Italian officers and soldiers were very good. People in Astypálaia enjoyed their freedom and took advantage of the infrastructures constructed by the Italians. The closer World War II came, the more the fascist regime of Mussolini oppressed the people.

It started forbidding the teaching of the Greek language before it completely banned it, as it also happened with Greek history and geography, while no Greek teachers were allowed on the island.

Typical postcard from the Italian occupation

They even tried to italicize the locals by founding a Catholic church. The relationships between the Greek inhabitants of the island and the Italian army deteriorated when the Greek-Italian war broke out in 1940. In any case, despite Mussolini's vain attempts to italicize the island, the interpersonal relationships of the locals with the Italians did not remind the relationship between a conqueror and a subject and all old locals remember with nostalgia those years; there are friendships that have survived to date.

The year 1943 found Italy defeated by the Allies and the Italian troops marooned on Astypálaia and the rest of the Dodecanese. The disagreement over the side they will support is now wide. In October 1943, after a controversial battle, the island is captured by their former German allies, who stay on the island until the end of the Third Reich, on May 8, 1945. The British, who take over after the Germans, are added to the long list of conquerors. In the conferences among the parts that participated in World War II held in Paris in 1946 and 1947, it is decided that Astypálaia and the rest of the Dodecanese will be annexed to Greece!

On March 31, 1947, the flag of Greece is raised in the castle of Astypálaia and the locals, wild with joy, welcome the Greek fleet and confer top honours! After so many centuries, Astypálaia returns to the lap of Mother Greece.

## "The Battle of Astypálaia"

In the summer of 1943 the Allies land on Sicily. The fascist regime of Italy collapses, Mussolini is ousted and General Badoglio assumes power. The general wants an agreement with the Allies, though without disturbing his relationship with Hitler. Germany answers with the occupation of the country. The war continues, with the Italian army being in the eye of the storm. This is also the case with the Italian troops in Astypálaia. The Germans have occupied Rhodes and Kos and are planning to attack Léros, which is the base of the Italian navy. The Italian administration both in Léros and Sámos has contacted the British and is determined to repel the German attack, which will only be successful as long as the Italian troops of Astypálaia are eliminated beforehand! But not all Italian officers and soldiers fully agree with the administration... On September 17, 1943, the military commander of the island, Margarucci, while cooperating with the British in view of the impending German attack, shoots down by mistake a British aircraft, which crashes at Agrelídi. At a later moment, while some German sailors from a ship sunk by allied vessels are captured on the north coasts, they rise in revolt with the silent consent of the Italian guard... The orders arriving from the Italian command of Léros with regard to the defence of the island are a little strange... The Italian-British command of Léros replaces Margarucci but that was not the end! At dawn of October 22, 1943, German Stukas bomb Astypálaia relentlessly! The 5 Italian batteries answered with only a few shots for honour's sake! The 4th Regiment of Bradenburgers (parachutists) falls in Maltezána, while an amphibious company of commandos lands on Pánormos. They meet heavy resistance from the Italian guard but they finally manage to overcome it. Parachutists also fall in Kaminákia. All German forces advance almost undisturbed and meet at Livádia. At 12 o' clock midday the "Battle of Astypálaia" has finished and some 700 Italian soldiers have surrendered. It is now the turn of the swastika to be raised in the castle...

*Luftwaffe over Astypálaia*

# FOLKLORE CULTURE

The active Cultural and Educational Association of Astypálaia is the guar-dian of the rich folklore tradition and culture of Astypálaia.

There are groups of traditional dances, a cloakroom with traditional costumes of Astypálaia, a lending library and a movie theatre (CINE AVRA). The association is responsible for the operation of the local radio station (RADIO MAMOUNI), pub-lishes a newspaper every two months (THE CASTLE OF ASTYPÁLAIA) and has the sports club of the island (Astypálaia F.C.) under its auspices, while it is the main contributor to all cultural events (KOUKANIA, MAXOULIA, Carnival).

Unfortunately, there is no indoor folklore museum so that the visitor can admire the traditional house of Astypálaia and the unique local costume! The plan for the operation of a folklore museum is under way, perhaps inside the castle, at "doctor's house," which has been restored.

### The Costume of Astypálaia

If you are lucky enough to visit Astypálaia during the cultural events, in which the dancing group of the Cultural Association takes part, you will admire the special and exquisite women's costume!

The costume of Astypálaia is one of the most fanciful of the Dodecanese because it has nothing in common with the costumes of the other islands. Made from valuable fabrics, full of embroidery work, gold and priceless gems, it is found in four versions: "chrysomántilo," "skléta," "ieró" and "misó." The two first are considered the richest of all; therefore, they are used mainly in weddings and engagements, while the third and the fourth are simpler.

"Chrysomántilo" is also called "skolo-pentráto" and consists of the following parts: The "tsopoukámiso" –a shirt with wide embroidered sleeves and a lower part with shapes of ships, birds, small camels with riders, trees and partridges, the "sleeved" dress, usually velvet in crimson or green colour, and the embroidered neckline with five-lira and other old and expensive gold coins ("konstantináta"). A special item of this costume is the "tsoúla," a triangular carved silver or golden plate with many little chains –small hanging little bells, which together with other items adorn the back of the costume. The "asiménio zonári" (silver belt) is worn around the waist, while the "armatosiá" is a golden or silver chain under the "zonári." At the edge of the "armatosiá" there are a perfume case and a little fish containing a needle, thread and a pair of scissors. The head is adorned with the famous golden stitched cap, which is no more worn today. High above, real pearls and colourful spar-kling stones on a wide band around the forehead, the "chryosomántilo," complete the lavishness and grace of this item.

A yellow silk scarf, finely stitched with golden threads, and the "panomoustouchiá" –a white silk scarf with embroidery work–, adorn the cap and are attached with two "karfovelónes" or "kombovelónes" – round balls with hanging fine chains and a variety of adornments, such as little fish, little birds, etc. The ears are adorned with carnations and "vérges" –long, pearl earrings. Finally, the costume includes the golden stitched "pasoúmia" (mules), which are accompanied with red golden stitched stockings.

---

*Text: Ioánna Mariáki, Photos: Ioánnis Lémis. Photo: Ioánna Mariáki and Giórgos Achladiótis*

The interior of a traditional house of Astypálaia drawn by A. Tarsoúli

## The Traditional House of Astypálaia

The houses inside the castle had only one space (one room). They were oblong, measuring approximately 6 x 3 m, and were very cleverly arranged since they took advantage of the limited space in order to meet all the basic needs of the family. The stove was in the front part (beside or under the window for better lighting). All side parts were full of shelves, where the people used to place their utensils, while the resting area was at the back.

The rear part was really adorable! A wooden complex structure was the resting area of the family.

The upper part, where the children slept, was called "sefás." The lower

Modern apartment according to the traditional architecture of the island (VIVA MARE apartments - Tel. No.: 0030-2243061571)

part, where the couple slept, was called "krévatos."

The two parts were divided by a wooden partition, the "tavládo." "Sefás" was covered with a woodcarving and "krévatos" with embroidered curtains, the "amousiés." The two parts communicated through a small door and wooden steps.

The rest whitewashed space under the "krévatos" was called "apokrévatos" and was used for storing food in "tzáres" (jars).

When the settlement expanded outside the castle, this type of single-space house acquired additional rooms and floors.

However, the main feature, which was the structure for the sleep of the family, remained!

Today there are some private houses and some rented rooms which have been arranged and decorated according to the traditional model.

## Music and Dance

Violin and lute! The soul of the Aegean music and indispensable accompaniment to any happy moment in Astypálaia.

Songs for weddings, engagements, love and, of course, songs for the castle and Panagiá Portaítissa! The traditional dances of bálos (in pairs m), soústa (in round dance m) and

### Traditional Song of Astypálaia

Portaítissa, my Lady, get out of Your chair,
To see the fun in Your yard.
Portaítissa, my Lady, with the big doors,
Take a look at our ships hanging around.
Portaítissa, my Lady, with Your only son,
See my love; he is in Your yard.
Panagiá Poularianí, You, who are in front of the cliffs,
See my love because my heart is trembling.
Aï-Giórgi (St. George) of the castle, with the silver hand,
Bring my love to be together.
Aï-Giórgi of the castle, with the golden spear,
Watch over my little bird so no one can steal it.
Ágie Giánni (St. John) tou Makrí, with the big faucet,
With the big heart and the cypress.
Ágie Giánni tou Makrí, with the long way,
Make me able to come five times a year.
At Agios Panteleímon, at the back of his dome,
I planted a lemon tree and I am on my way to water it.
To a celebration we went, at Agios Konstantínos,
I wish His grace allows us to reach Tínos!

karsilamás (in pairs m) are danced here as in all Aegean Islands, though in the particular way of Astypálaia!

## "Koukánia"

Koukánia

Athletic events held every year on August 16 on the beach of Péra Gialós by the Cultural Association with the participation of all the young of the island. The participants compete in tug-of-war, sack races, egg races, "blind" eating of yogurt, and "peteinós" (rooster)! The last of them is very much fun: a horizontal pole is extended over the sea after it has been covered with grease while a basket including a dummy rooster is hanging from the edge of the pole. The winner should walk along the greased pole and catch the rooster without falling into the sea!

If you happen to be on that date in Astypálaia, do not miss "Koukánia"! You will really enjoy it!

## Astypálaia Festival and "Maxoúlia"

Every July and August the Municipality of Astypálaia and the Cultural Association hold several cultural events.

Theatrical performances, concerts, music-dance performances, photography and painting exhibitions. You can find posters and prospectuses informing about the place and time of the events.

**Radio "Mamoúni" at 106.00 FM!**

# ECONOMY

Local economy is mainly based on tourism, which has shown a rapid development in recent years.

Over 100 tourist spots (hotels, rooms to rent, campsite) with approximately 1,500 beds operate on the island. Most of the seasonal local workforce is employed in catering, entertainment and accommodation facilities.

Agriculture is not particularly developed in Astypálaia due to the semi-mountainous land. However, local agricultural products are enough to

Apiculture and stock-breeding are among the main activities of the locals

cover the demand. Barley, vegetables, mandarins as well as top quality potatoes and sweet potatoes are produced in the flat areas of Livádi, Maltezána and Vathý. Stock-breeding holds the main part of the primary sector.

More than 12,000 sheep and goats graze in the pasturelands of the mountains and in nearby islets.

Apiculture also holds a significant position, with 3,000 beehives scattered all around the island, which produce exceptional honey (already known from antiquity) with a high content of fragrant thyme grains.

As it happens with all Aegean islands, the locals are also involved with the sea. There are about 100 amateur and professional fishing boats, while floating fish farms exist at Vái and on the islet of Lignós.

Apiculture and stock-breeding are among the main activities of the locals

# SETTLEMENTS

There are four settlements on the island: Análipsi (or Maltezána), Vathý, Livádi and Chóra (Péra Gialós).

## Análipsi or Maltezána

It is situated almost in the middle of the strip of land connecting the two wings of the butterfly, within 10 km from Chóra, 6 km from the port of Agios Andréas, and less than 1 km from the airport of the island. Some 150 people live in the village, which was named after an old chu-rch that existed in the area and was dedicated to the Análipsi (the Ascension of Jesus), while the name Maltezána comes from the Maltese pirates that used the closed cove as a base be-tween the 16th and the 18th c. it is built in a verdant area full of orchards, in a scenic little cove surrounded by the little islets of Hondró and Lignó.

Until a few years ago the settle-ment was a rural fishing village but the calm atmosphere and the splen-did sandy beach with the tamarisks have turned the place into a tourist

The holiday resort of Schoinóntas

View of Análipsi from the sea

View of Análipsi from the area of the airport

The restaurant of "Galíni" at the quay of the little settlement

resort with modern infrastructures. In Maltezána you can see the Roman Baths of Talará, the Early Christian basilicas of Agia Varvára and Karékli, and the monument of the killed French sailors and Captain Bisson in Schinóntas, while equally impressive are the foundations of ancient houses on the seabed at the west edge of the beach.

The two wonderful traditional cafes on the main alley and the original fish taverns along the coast to Schinóntas, which is the natural continuation of Maltezána, will give you the chance to have a break and try Aegean tastes! There are two mini-markets.

The limekiln at Vathý is a monument of past times...

## Vathý

The smallest settlement of the island with only 15 permanent inhabitants! It is divided into Éxo Vathý (outer), at the deepest point of the fjord formed in the north part of the island (1 family), and Mésa Vathý (inner), on the north beach of the namesake cove, 1.5 km after Éxo Vathý. The distance from Chóra is approximately 20 km.

The 10 km from Maltezána are dirt road (quite trafficable) but asphalt surfacing works are in progress. The name in Greek means deep due to the sea that advances deep into the land like a fjord (a feature common in other islands of the same morphology as well, such as Kálymnos and Sífnos). In the past there were several inhabitants, who worked at the nearby lime kilns, but the settlement was gradually abandoned. Today there are only a few houses along the coast of Mésa Vathý and cottages in Éxo Vathý.

In the wider area the visitor can admire the famous rock paintings as well as ruins of a Minoan settlement. The tranquillity and absolute silence prevailing in the lagoon will reward you. The only little tavern operating in the quay of Mésa Vathý is called "Galíni" (tranquillity). There is no accommodation or shops here.

The "lost lake" from the hill of Agios Nikólaos

Livádi

## Livádi

The place took this name (meadow in Greek) because it is the flat and most fertile area of the island. It is situated in Éxo Nisí, to the south and very close to Chóra (1 km), and has a population of 110. The waters from the springs as well as the artificial lake to the NW are responsible for the existence of orchards, which offer the area its green colour.

The main road crossing the settlement is actually the torrent coming from the dam, which branches among the orchards and the mandarin trees. The visitor can find here plenty of rooms to rent, while the beautiful pebbled beach is organized and full of restaurants, cafes, bars and shops, and offers a beautiful view of the castle of Chóra.

The plain of Livádi

A pretty house in Chóra

## Chóra and Péra Gialós

The capital of the island. If not the prettiest (in my opinion, it is), this is one of the prettiest capitals in the Aegean! A real painting regardless of where you look at it from, at any time, day or night! Péra Gialós (or Skála) is part of Chóra but it is mentioned separately because it has a different morphology.

The population amounts to 1,055. It is situated to the SE (in Éxo Nisí), within 6 km from the port of AGIOS Andréas and 10 km from the airport. The history of the place is identified with the history of the whole island. This has always been the heart of Astypálaia.

Chóra is built on the hill below the castle, on the saddle between the castle and the hill of Profítis Ilías, on the slope below the saddle and down to the cove of Péra Gialós. There are certain parts, from a specific point on the hill of the castle (on all sides) down to the sea, which have not been built up so that this amazing view can remain unharmed. All public services and most of the shops and tourist infrastructures of the island are here. The visitor can also see the most important places of the island: the castle, the windmills, the church of Panagia Portaítissa, the archaeological museum and the infant cemetery, though one should never forget that the entire settle-

The church of Megáli Panagía with the pebbled floor

The road to the left of the Town Hall leads to Megáli Panagía

ment of Chóra is a place of interest of its own! It includes 8 quarters or municipal districts. The 6 of them are in the old settlement around the castle, where there are no services but only a few shops: Karái, Megáli Panagiá, Pálos, Papadáki, Asvestotí and Portaítissa. Two main roads open up in front of the town hall and enclose the entire old settlement. Follow either of them and you will get lost in the narrow alleys and the white steps that meander through this fantastic village! The road to the left crosses the quarter of Karái –to the NW of the castle-, where you can admire the complex of the 6+3 successive little churches (Pródromos, AGIOS Paraskeví, Lemonítria, Aï-Stratigós, Orthodoxía, Panagia Orfanoú +Treis Ierárches, Agioi Pántes, Anonymous)! Then the road crosses the quarter of Megáli Panagiá with the namesake 18th c. church and its wonderful pebbled yard.

The chapel of Agios Nikólaos is attached to the south partition wall of Megáli Panagiá.

Take a break at Kástro café-bar and enjoy the wonderful view! The road to the right (to the south of the castle) runs in front of the town hall and crosses the quarters of Pálos, Papadáki and Asvestotí before it

The road to the right of the Town Hall leads to the castle and Portaítissa

The centre of Chóra

ends at the complex of Panagia Portaítissa. The quarter of the town hall is the centre of Chóra and is built on the flat area around the town hall. It was built in 1946 on the site of 6 small churches.

There used to be 9, just like in Karái, but only 3 of them have survived at the back of the town hall to the hill of Profítis Ilías. The 8 traditional windmills are built on the saddle between the two hills and above the central square of Chóra, where you can find traditional cafes, modern cafes, taverns and shops.

On the square stands the Narkísseios municipal library, which was named after the benefactor priest Father Nárkissos Morfinós, and the war memorial. The area of the windmills is the main junction of the island.

Péra Gialós is built on the slope of the saddle between the hills of Chóra and beside the seashore! It is the second biggest and oldest port of the island. Along the small organized beach of the cove you can find the archaeological museum as well as several restaurants, cafes and shops.

A building from the period of the Italian occupation accommodates the bank, the police station, the port authorities and the customs. Wherever you choose to have your meal or coffee, the view of the hill of the castle is magnificent!

Péra Gialós

# SIGHTS

Despite its small size, Astypálaia has several sights to see. Here are the most important of them:

## The Castle

It is undoubtedly the emblem of the island! What you see today is the remains of the Venetian castle of the Querini Family after it was restored by Giovanni IV Querini in 1413. However, according to archaeologists, there has always been a fortified structure on this location since the 8th c. BC. This means that the Venetians built their castle on the foundations of a Byzantine castle, which was built on the site of a Roman castle, which was built on the ancient Greek acropolis! It stands 130 m above sea level and was inhabited until 1948! The walls of the castle are the exterior walls of the houses that formed the fortified (for the fear of pirates) settlement. In an area of only 0.4 hectares lived approximately 1000 people (when the island was under siege all the inhabitants

The Castle of Astypálaia

The tower of Saray from Portaítissa

"Ksókastra" (outside the castle) houses

of Astypálaia entered the castle!)! How could such a thing happen? The houses that formed the walls had three floors and each of them had a main space.

The houses inside the castle were also very small and several of them had more than one floor. They were terraced houses, with very few free spaces and extremely narrow alleys instead of roads. In the period when the castle was the main (and quite often the only) settlement of the island, the buildings inside the castle covered more than 90% of the area!

The maximum height of the walls is 14 m and the approximate width 1 m, while there were several defensive loopholes. The houses inside the walls also served as abutments that improved the static sufficiency of the overall fortification. Like every other castle with towers, the castle of Astypálaia has two towers necessary for its defence: a four-story tower to the south, exactly above Portaítissa Monastery, which is called Sarái (it is easily understood that it accommodated the Ottoman commander during the Turkish occupation), and, of course, the tower at the gate of the castle, whose complex includes the church of Panagia of the castle.

There is only one gate deliberately built at a very narrow point so that the enemy cannot gather too many men for the attack. As soon as you walk through the double castle door, you enter a space covered with two groined vaults.

Above the vaults stands Panagia of the castle. It is a church with a blue dome visible from outside the castle, which was built in 1853 to serve as cathedral. However, the construction of the church required the prior demolition of the upper part of the tower of the gate, which was the house of the Querini Family. The church is dedicated to the Annunciation. The south side accommodates the church of Agios Geórgios. It was built in 1790 and the area in front of the church served as the square of the fortified town, the so-called blátsa. The inte-

Ruins to the NW of the castle

Panagiá of the castle from inside the walls

rior of the castle and the "doctor's house," which has been restored, are open to visitors. The wood-carved ceiling of the house is really impressive!

Apart from the churches and a couple of buildings, the interior of the castle is in ruins due to the mighty earthquake of 1956 that struck Astypálaia and the habit of the earlier inhabitants of demolishing their houses, when they abandoned the castle after the early 19th c., in order to use the materials in the new buildings they would construct outside the castle.

The castle is open to visitors from 08:00 to 14:00 and from 16:30 to 18:30; admission is free and the girl at the entrance will be very helpful with your visit.

## The Windmills

The windmills are the second most characteristic sight of Astypálaia. They used to mill grain taking advantage of the abundant Aeolian power produced on the saddle between the two hills of Chóra.

Similar windmills can be found in several Aegean Islands but these are in a very good condition (restored) and match perfectly the landscape of Astypálaia.

When they operated both the roofs and the sails were constructed in a way that they always turned to the direction of the wind.

The exact date of construction is unknown. The windmills have a horizontal axis and vertical sails that can

Agios Geórgios o Glykavlís

The cute lending library for foreigners inside one of the windmills

be turned manually through a special arrangement that follows the direction of the wind (this is the type that prevails in the Aegean Islands). They appeared during the Frankish occupation (13th and 14th c.). There are 8 windmills dominating the saddle of Chóra, while the one nearest to the castle is private and accommodates the namesake ("mý-los" meaning mill in Greek) mini market and a newsstand. The rest of them belong to the Archaeological Service and accommodate a lending library with foreign language books and the municipal tourist agency. The area around the windmills is the heart of Chóra!

The windmills. The second trademark of the island!

The Infant Cemetery

## The Infant Cemetery!

To the SW of the hill of the castle you can see (even from a long distance) some strange square hollows in the ground.

The area is called Kylíndra and is an archaeological site with no impressive buildings but with very impressive finds! It is an ancient infant cemetery unique in the whole world that was discovered in 1995 following the foundation works for a building. The 12th Ephorate of Antiquities that excavates the area has brought to light the remains of almost 3,000 infants inside cauldrons!

The dead bodies were put inside cauldrons or vessels because these items resembled the female womb and, therefore, the souls of the dead infants could feel the safety of the mother. The infants were aged from a few days to a few months old and the finds cover a long period from the 7th to the 2nd c. BC. It seems that in ancient years Astypálaia was a sacred place and accepted prematurely dead infants from all the Greek world of the east Mediterranean. This is evidenced by the large numbers of vessels with infants that come from different areas of the Greek mainland, the Aegean Islands, Asia Minor, even from Palestine! Probably there was a sanctuary dedicated to Eileíthyia and Locheía Ártemis (goddesses protecting the pains of birth) in the area.

Access to visitors is prohibited and the only thing one can see is the excavation works. Finds are exhibited at the archaeological museum as well as in a space specially created inside the old high school in Péra Gialós.

## Archaeological Museum

It is situated in Péra Gialós, in a small building where the finds are neatly exhibited in chronological order, covering the period from the Prehistoric Period

(2800 BC) to the Middle Ages as well as the period of the Venetian occupation (1500 AD).

Amphorae, daggers, jewels, burial offerings from tombs, coins, figurines, inscriptions and, of course, a hydría including the remains of an infant from Kylíndra are some of the exhibits you can admire in the small, though rich, museum of Astypálaia.

Admission is free and opening hours are Tuesday to Saturday from 08:00 to 20:00 and on Sunday and Monday from 09:00 to 15:00. Information: (0030) 2243061500.

## Talará Roman Baths

They are situated in Análipsi, almost behind the church of Agios Dimítrios, but have not been developed. The floor was covered with a mosaic depicting Time who is holding Earth in his hand.

The figure is surrounded by the signs of the zodiac. It was made in the Late Roman period (4th c. AD).

## Monument of French Sailors

It is situated at Schoinóntas, at the tip of the peninsula extending to the left of the beach. The monument was erected by the French Navy in honour of the killed sailors and Captain Bisson, who commanded the corvette "Lamproire" and the commandeered piratical ship "Panagiótis." On November 5, 1827, the two ships were sailing in the sea of Maltezána and the captain chose to blow his

Hydria-Kalpis that included a dead infant

The monument of the French sailors at Schoinóntas

ship up instead of surrendering to the pirates that had attacked him. 15 French sailors and 60 pirates were killed. The monument denotes self-sacrifice against the piracy that bedeviled the Aegean until the first half of the 19th c.

## Paliókastro

Ruins of a Byzantine castle situated on the SW side of the island, on an idyllic spot, in the area of Aï-Giánnis o Makrýs. It is the fortress-stro-nghold of Astypálaia, where all locals sought refuge during enemy raids in the Byzantine period.

The fortress was captured and ruined by the notorious pirate Barbarossa in 1537.Although access is quite difficult, the area is worth visiting due to its special natural beauty.

The ruins of the Byzantine Paliókastro at Aï-Giánnis

# THE CHURCH

The churches of Astypálaia should form an independent chapter because they are real architectural monuments and because the locals have fostered close relations with Orthodoxy.

Astypálaia is directly under the jurisdiction of the Ecumenical Patriarchate of Constantinople and belongs to the administration of the bishopric of Kálymnos, Léros and Astypálaia.

## Portaítissa

The church of the old monastery of Panagia Portaítissa, which is the most famous church of the island, is situated to the south of the hill of the castle, on the location of Rodiá. It was built in 1762 by Ósios (saint) Ánthimos of Kefaloniá, who is also the patron saint of the island.

The thaumaturgic icon of Panagia Portaítissa is a replica of the name-

Panagiá Portaítissa (the Virgin)

The thaumaturgic icon of Portaítissa

sake icon of Ivíron Monastery in Mt. Athos. According to holy tradition, Ánthimos was born in Lixoúri of Kefaloniá in 1727 and at the age of 7 he was blinded by smallpox.

When he came of age, he became a monk in Mt. Athos and, not before long, he started his missionary activities. The islands of the archipelago, where he preached the teachings of Jesus, gave him the title of "the blind missionary of the Aegean." Chíos, Sífnos, Páros, Náxos, Síkinos, Kýthira, Crete and Kastelórizo are only some of the islands he visited and founded 6 monasteries! In 1761 Ánthimos arrived in Astypálaia, where he wanted to build the third successive monastery and dedicate it to Panagia (the Virgin). When the construction of the monastery was near completion, the saint decided to adorn it with an icon of the Virgin. Therefore, he went to Mt. Athos, where he found a very old monk-iconographer and requested him to paint an icon as beautiful as that of Ivíron Monastery. But the old man fell sick and was unable to finish the icon. According to holy tradition, a miracle happened at the time. The icon was completed by itself and Ánthimos happily brought it back to Astypálaia and placed it in the monastery church.

The monastery operated as a nunnery. It was proclaimed stauropegian and was subjected directly to the Ecumenical Patriarchate, but the time it stopped operating as a monastery is unknown. Apart from the "katholikón" (main church), which is a domed basilica dedicated to the Koímisi tis Theotókou (the Passing of the Virgin), the complex also includes two chapels (Agios Stéfanos and Agios Dimítrios) as well as some

The Byzantine grandeur is evident inside the church

Exceptional painting inside the Monastery

auxiliary structures. The marble bell tower and the 18th c. wood-carved iconostasis are very impressive. The ecclesiastical museum with the holy heirlooms from the entire island (icons, ornaments, canonicals, gospels) is also accommodated here.

A 17th c. epitáphios (liturgical cloth placed on a wooden structure and symbolizing the funeral shroud of Jesus) will catch your eye. Apart from the thaumaturgic icon of Panagia Portaítissa, the visitor can also see the right forearm of Ósios Ánthimos. Portaítissa celebrates on August 15, when the greatest religious feast of the island takes place. Live music, dance and much fun until late at night in the yard of the monastery, where local traditional dishes and plenty of wine are served!

## Early Christian Basilicas

Basilicas were public buildings used for public gatherings in Roman years. After the 4th c. they adapted to the needs of the Christian population of the empire, which was steadily on the increase.

They are typical examples of Early Christian architecture. The basilicas of Astypálaia include some very interesting mosaic floors.

***Ágios Vassíleios:*** to the right of a peninsula next to Livádi.

Agía Varvára: in Análipsi, on a hill to the north of the settlement. You'll have to open and close the wooden gate (for the animals) that you'll find on the dirt road. It has allegedly been built on the site of a temple of Ártemis.

***Kareklí:*** in the wider area of Maltezána, shortly after the monument of the French sailors at Schoinóntas: although surrounded with fence, you can admire the superb mosaics.

Agios Dimítrios in Análipsi

Old Monasteries, Country Churches and Celebrations

According to local folk tradition, Astypálaia has 365 little churches, a number equal to the days of the year! Because this belief is repeated in several Aegean Islands, it must be untrue. It just shows the increased religiousness of the locals.

In any case, the approximately 200 country churches, main churches and chapels are not a small number! Besides, most of them are amazing! The most important in the Orthodox tradition of Astypálaia are:

***Flevariótissa:*** an old monastery in Éxo Nisí, within 7 km from Chóra. Built in a beautiful valley, it is inactive, just like Portaítissa, and celebrates on February 2, on the day of the Hypapante, when the locals hold a great winter religious celebration.

It is named after February. From the junction on the dirt road, to your right, you can see the monastery behind the locked railed gate.

The shepherd-guard of the monastery is usually around and when you call him, he will open the door for you. Padlocks are used because the monastery has repeatedly been robbed! In the chapel, which is carved inside the cliff and has been included in the main church, the visitor can see an icon of the Virgin reading "Agía Libýi" (Saint Libya).

***Aï-Giánnis o Makrýs:*** another old and inactive monastery situated in one of the most beautiful places of Astypálaia (within approximately 10 km from Chóra), to the west of Éxo Nisí and opposite Paliókastro.

It is an absolutely idyllic setting! The word Makrýs means long. The monastery is dedicated to St. John the Baptist and celebrates on August 29.

***Panagiá Poularianí:*** a very picturesque country church situated just before Poúlaris Cape, to the east of Mésa Nisí. The picture of the Virgin with the Holy Baby is formed on the rock. It is considered the patron saint of the sailors and lies within almost 20 km from Chóra. It is dedicated to the birthday of the Virgin and celebrates on September 8.

***Panagía tou Thomá:*** an equally beautiful country church on the north side of Mésa Nisí, within 25 km from

Panagiá tou Thomá (the Virgin)

Panagiá Poulariani (the Virgin)

Aï-Giánnis o Makrýs and Anáfi in the background!

AGIOU IOANNOU
PRODROMOU

Chóra. It was named after the mountain, which is called Agios Thomás, and also celebrates on the Virgin's birthday, on September 8. A great feast is held with traditional live music and plenty of food!

Other churches holding religious celebrations are Agios Dimítrios in Maltezána on October 26, Agios Nikólaos in Péra Gialós on December 6, Agios Panteleímon, at the namesake little church in the area of Armenochóri of Éxo Nisí, on July 27, and Metamórfosi (the Transfiguration), at the little church beside the dam in Livádi, on August 6.

A great religious celebration in Astypálaia is the day dedicated to the memory of its patron saint Ánthimos, on September 4.

## The E.C.F.A.

The Ecclesiastical Charity Fund of Astypálaia has made a huge social contribution. It was established in 1820 in order to deal, among others, with the needs of Greek education in the Ottoman-occupied Astypálaia. According to its Articles, all the inhabitants of the island are members of the Fund. The revenues come from donations and endowments as well as from the commercial exploitation of the approximately 4,000 hectares it possesses, including pastureland and the respective pens the Fund hires to local stock-breeders. The Fund aims at financially aiding poor families, granting scholarships to poor young people, endowing poor girls (in earlier times) and, generally, promoting the spiritual, cultural and religious activities of the people of Astypálaia.

Flevariótissa (the Virgin)

# ROUTES OF THE ISLAND

When someone comes to Astypálaia for the first time and sees the arid and barren landscape, one may think that, apart from the evident destinations (Chóra, Livádi, Maltezána) that are connected through the asphalt road, there are possibly no other reasons why one should experience hardships to see the rest of the island. Well, you'd better think it twice! Reddish mountains, green valleys, a waterfall, a lake, monasteries, scenic country churches, amazing caves, a fjord, an unbelievable view of the Aegean and the nearby islands as well as dozens of beaches are what the visitors see on the island. You are bound to be really amazed. Due to the morphology of the island and the road network the tour of Astypálaia will be divided into three routes. The starting point is always Chóra.

**ATTENTION!** WHILE WALKING OR DRIVING IN THE INTERIOR OF ASTYPÁLAIA, YOU WILL OFTEN FIND WOODEN GATES ALONG DIRT ROADS. DO NOT WORRY. THEY DO NOT INTEND TO PREVENT YOU FROM CONTINUING YOUR WAY. THEY JUST BLOCK THE ROAD TO SHEEP AND GOATS SO THAT THEY CANNOT LEAVE THE SPECIFIC AREA. OPEN THE GATE, WALK OR DRIVE THROUGH, AND THEN DO NOT FORGET TO CLOSE IT AGAIN!

Ακ.Φλούδα
C. Flouda
Σπήλαιο Δράκου (Δρακοσπηλιά)
Drakou Cave (Drakospilia)
ΠΑΝΑΓΙΑ ΤΟΥ ΘΩΜΑ
PANAGIA TOU THOMA
Έξω Βαθύ
Exo Vathi
Μέσα Βαθύ
Mesa Vathi
Μπούκα - Bouka
N. ΦΩΚΙΑ
FOKIA ISL.
ΦΩΚΟΝΗΣΙΑ
FOKONISIA
N. ΑΓ. ΝΙΚΟΛΑΟΣ
AG. NIKOLAOS ISL.
N. ΜΑΞΙΛΑΡΙ
MAXILARI ISL.
Όρμος Βαγίπ
Vagi Bay
Μεγάλο Βάι
Megalo Vai B.
Π. ψιλή Άμμος
Κρατικός Αερολιμένας Αστυπάλαιας
National Airport of Astypalaia
Σχοινώντας
Schoinontas
Όρμος Άγ. Ανδρέα
Ag. Andreas Bay
Ανάληψη (Μαλτεζάνα)
Analipsi (Maltezana)
Μνημείο Γάλλων Ναυτικών
Monument of French Navy
Π. Βρύσι
Vrissi B.
Όρμος Στενό
Steno Bay
Όρμος Μαρμάρι
Marmari Bay
N. ΛΙΓΝΟ
LIGNO ISL.
Πέρα Γιαλός
Pera Gialos
Λιβάδι
Livadi
Χώρα
Chora
N. ΑΓ. ΚΥΡΙΑΚΗ
AG. KYRIAKI ISL.
Όρμος Λιβάδι
Livadi Bay

Προτεινόμενη Διαδρομή
Recommended Route
Percorso Consigliato
Ν. ΑΣΤΥΠΑΛΑΙΑ
ASTYPALAIA ISL.
Π. Ζαφείρι
Zafiri B.
Αγ. Νικόλαος
Ag. Nikolaos
Κτίρια
ΜΟΜΑ
Καστελάνος
Kastelanos
(366 m.)
ΠΑΝΑΓΙΑ ΠΟΥΛΑΡΙΑΝΗ
PANAGIA POULARIANI
Αγρελίδι
Agrelidi
Όρμος Βλυχάδια
Vlichadia Bay
Π. Αγρελίδι
Agrelidi B.
Ακ. Πούλαρης
C. Poularis
Όρμος Άγ. Φωκά
Ag. Fokas Bay
Ν. ΚΟΥΤΣΟΜΥΤΗΣ
KOUTSOMYTIS ISL.
Ν. ΤΗΓΑΝΙ
TIGANI ISL.
Ν. ΜΟΝΗ
MONI ISL.
Ν. ΦΤΕΝΟ
FTENO ISL.
Ν. ΚΟΥΝΟΥΠΟΙ
KOUNOUPOI ISL.
Ν. ΧΟΝΔΡΟΠΟΥΛΟ
HONDROPOULO ISL.

The beach of the campsite at Marmári

## Mésa Nisí

Follow the ring road and, after bypassing Péra Gialós, you reach the coast in the cove of Marmári. To the right you can see three successive beaches with the same name. In Marmári B (with the tamarisks) there is a campsite. A little ahead, the road runs uphill to the left and after a while you get to a junction. The left road leads to the port of Agios Andréas and the right to Análipsi and Mésa Nisí.

You turn right and not before long you reach a church (Stavroú). Now you are at the narrowest point of the isthmus of Astypálaia (105 m). To the right there are two beautiful beaches called "Stenó," with the second one being larger and organized. The next beach is the popular "Plákes" (there is a sign). If you continue along the asphalt road, you will find the junction to the Airport to the left. The road, apart from the airport, also runs to the north beach of Chrysí Ámmos. Continue straight and enter the settlement of Análipsi (see p.43). I would suggest a visit to the basilica of Agia Varvára (see p.71) and a coffee break at one of the two pretty cafes, Maltézos and Marínos. Then you get to the beach of Maltezána.

The beach of Stenó

Follow the coastal road and, after a while, you enter the settlement of Schoinóntas with the sandy beach and the tamarisks to the right and the fishing boats to the left.

Towards the end of the beach you will find a sign to the right, which shows the way to the monument of the French sailors (see p.65) at the tip of the peninsula. The distance to get there is only 300 m. If you turn right at the previous sign, the asphalt ends after a few metres. The sign says that asphalt surfacing works as far as Vathý are in progress. That's true and you can verify it by yourself. The works are to be completed until 2017. However, the main dirt road can be accessed even by small cars. After almost 1 km to the left you can see a narrow and quite rough dirt road that leads to the beach of Psilí Ámmos as well as to the beaches of Megálo Vái and Mikró Vái (approx. 1 km and 3 km) with the fish farms. A small settlement that was completely devastated by the 1956 earthquake used to be to the north of the middle of the road running from Megálo Vái to Mikró Vái. There is nothing worth seeing on this side of the island. You are now at the end of the isthmus of the "butterfly." Continue along the main dirt road and after 3.5 km you can see a sign to the right showing the way to Agrelídi. The distance is less than 500 m and you should not miss it. You reach a closed and calm cove called Porto Agrelídi.

On the beach to the left you can see some ruins. Until some decades ago there was a small settlement here with people working at the industrial limekiln. The little church you see on the cliffs is Agios Nikólaos. Return to the main road and turn right. The road starts running uphill and after 2 km you get to a crossroads with old military buildings all around.

The bay of Agrelídi

Turn right and go uphill to the peak of Kastelános (366 m), the highest mountain of Mésa Nísi. After 1,100 m you can see to the left a narrow dirt road that leads to the flat area of the top with the antennas.

You do not have to walk up there as the view is wonderful from this point as well! As long as the atmosphere is clear, you can see the west coasts of Kos to the NE and Kálymnos a little to the left, while in the opposite direction, the entire bulk of Astypálaia emerges together with the nearby islets.

The strange cement fortification structures all around were made by the Italian army and served as cannon

The peak of Kastelános

The view of Éxo Nisí from Kastelános is majestic

bases. If you continue, the road runs downhill and, after 2 km, you reach at the end, where you can see the scenic yet inactive monastery-country church of Panagiá Poularianí (see p.72).

The namesake promontory below is the easternmost point of the island. Now return to the old military structures. Turn right in the direction of Vathý. To the right, after approximately 1 km, you can see down below the steep and wonderful beach of Zafeirianí, while the little church of Panagia is a little higher.

Do not even imagine going down the beach, no matter how much you want it, because the only access is through the sea. Continue your way along the main dirt road and, after about 2 km, you reach Éxo Vathý.

There is farmed land at the deepest point of the fjord and a family of farmers live permanently here.

When you stand right at the deepest point of the cove, you can see the hill with the little church of Agios Nikólaos to the left. The view of the cove is superb but you are not advised to go up there unless you have the right car. From this point it looks like a lagoon.

Besides, apart from Vathý Cove, it is also called "The Lost Lake"! After you pass Éxo Vathý, continue along the coast to the opening of the cove and, after the abandoned limekiln, you reach the little settlement of Mésa Vathý.

At the quay you will find the cafe-restaurant Galíni (tranquility), which

The old monastery of Poularianí

The beautiful beach of Zafeirianí on the way to Vathý

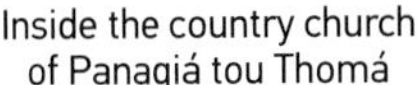
Inside the country church of Panagiá tou Thomá

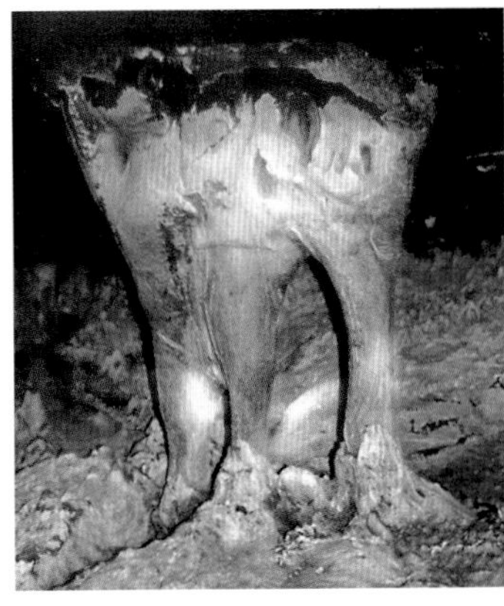
Drakou Cave

definitely justifies its name! Enjoy the absolute silence and tranquility. As it happened in Agrelídi, there were many more inhabitants in the past, who worked in lime production.

Rock paintings from the Prehistoric and Classical years were found on the coast opposite the quay, while at the entrance of "Boúka," as the channel is called, the ruins of a Hellenistic tower were found. The route in Mésa Nisí ends at the monastery of Panagia tou Thomá.

Continue along the dirt road after Mésa Vathý by turning right and going up a distance of approximately 2.5 km. You reach the old little monastery (see p.72). The view of the north bay of Astypálaia is wonderful. The large numbers of wild rabbits will amaze you! A goat path to the north of the church leads close to the beautiful cave of Drákou after 1,600 m!

The cave is situated in a cove formed by the northernmost cape of the island, the Floúda. Access from land is dangerous and should be avoided.

You had better go by sea in case you have a vessel. It is a really amazing cave with stalagmites and stalactites but it has not been fully explored yet. Visitors should be extremely careful.

The bay at Vathý from above. The little settlement in Mésa Vathý is to the left.

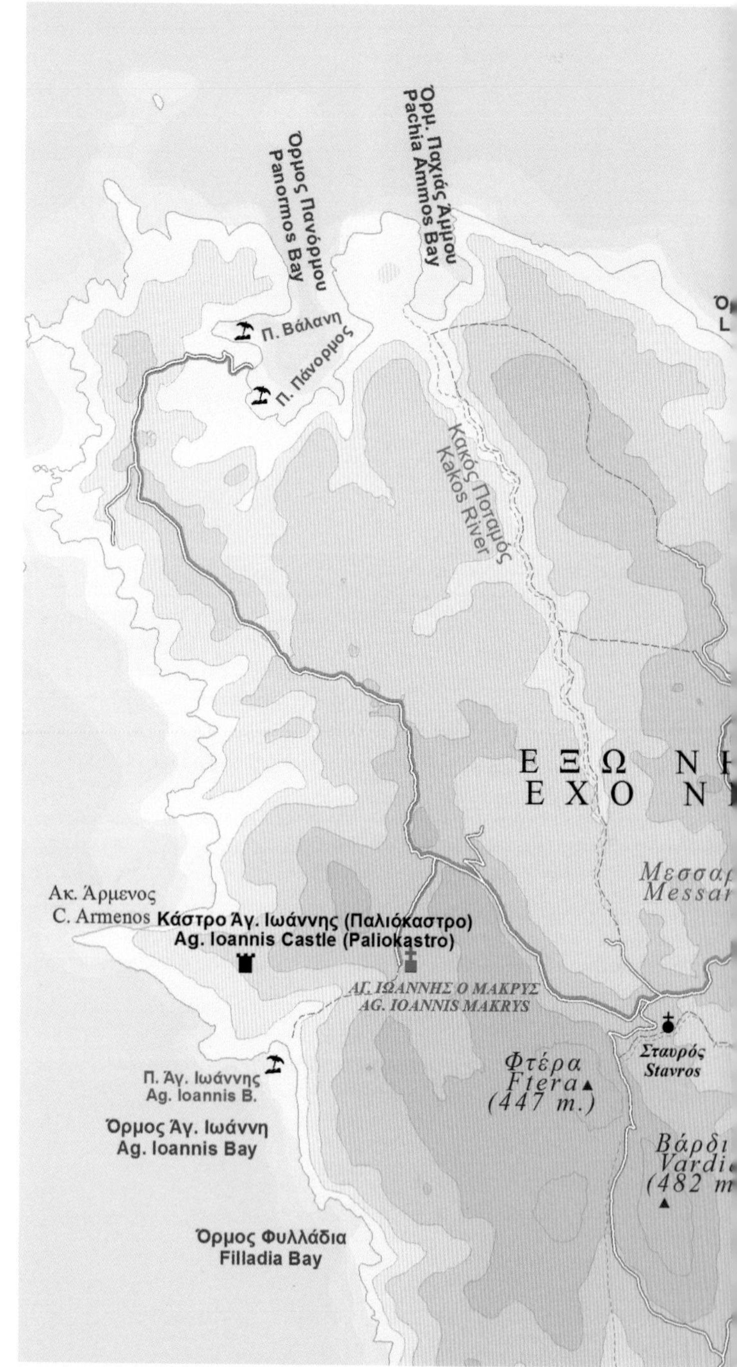
Όρμος Πανόρμου
Panormos Bay
Όρμ. Παχιάς Άμμου
Pachia Ammos Bay
Π. Βάλανη
Π. Πάνορμος
Κακός Ποταμός
Kakos River
Ε Ξ Ω
Ε Χ Ο
Ακ. Άρμενος
C. Armenos
Κάστρο Άγ. Ιωάννης (Παλιόκαστρο)
Ag. Ioannis Castle (Paliokastro)
ΑΓ. ΙΩΑΝΝΗΣ Ο ΜΑΚΡΥΣ
AG. IOANNIS MAKRYS
Σταυρός
Stavros
Φτέρα
Ftera
(447 m.)
Π. Άγ. Ιωάννης
Ag. Ioannis B.
Όρμος Άγ. Ιωάννη
Ag. Ioannis Bay
Όρμος Φυλλάδια
Filladia Bay

Προτεινόμενη Διαδρομή
Recommended Route
Percorso Consigliato
Ν. ΑΓ. ΝΙΚΟΛΑΟΣ
AG. NIKOLAOS ISL.
ΦΩΚΟΝΗΣΙΑ
FOKONISIA
Ν. ΜΑΞΙΛΑΡΙ
MAXILARI ISL.
Όρμ. Λιμανάρι
Limanari Bay
Όρμος Άγ. Ανδρέα
Ag. Andreas Bay
ΠΑΝΑΓΙΑ ΦΛΕΒΑΡΙΩΤΙΣΣΑ
PANAGIA FLEVARIOTISSA
Τεχνητή Λίμνη
Artificial Lake
Άγ. Βασίλειος
Ag. Vassilios
Πέρα Γιαλός
Pera Gialos
Λιβάδι
Livadi
Χώρα
Chora
Άγ. Βασίλειος
Ag. Vassilios
Π. Λιβάδι
Livadi B.
Όρμος Λιβάδι
Livadi Bay

## North Éxo Nisí

From the main junction at Chóra follow the road (there is a relevant sign) to Flevariótissa and Agios Ioánnis. After a while the asphalt ends but the dirt road is quite trafficable. Go up the hill of Profítis Ilías, opposite Chóra, and continue to the next hill that embraces Chóra. From high above the view is wonderful as this is one of the ideal spots of the island if you want to take pictures! Not before long the road turns left and you cannot see Chóra anymore. However, as soon as you reach the level of the mobile telephony antennas, you start having an amazing view of the plain of Livádi and the artificial lake. Continue along the main dirt road for another 3 km.

Before you reach the junction to Flevariótissa Monastery (there is a relevant sign), you will see two dirt roads to the right of your way, which lead to two country churches –the first to Agia Triáda and the second to Agia Marína– and to some pens. Shortly after the heliport and the antennas, turn right to the direction indicated by the sign.

Follow the quite trafficable dirt road for 1,700 m while you catch a glimpse of the north bay of the island to your right.

You reach a fork from where you can see the monastery of Panagia Flevariótissa to the right and down the slope, behind a metal railed gate (see p.72).

Straight ahead the road leads to the country church of Panagia ton Vryssón. The first path to the beach of Pachiá Ámmos, in the north part of the island, starts from this point and the second starts 300 m before the first. The route returns from Flevariótissa to the main dirt road and then turns right to Aï-Giánnis o Makrýs.

View of Chóra from Paliómylos (old mill)

The breathtaking view from the roa to Aï-Giánnis is like a real painting

Cross the plateau of Messariá (at the centre of Éxo Nisí) for two kilometers and reach the crossroads of Stavroú. To the left the road runs uphill to the little church of Stavroú and the mountain tops of Várdia, while to the right there is a minor fork leading to the church of Agioi Pántes. Immediately after that, slightly to the right, you find Agios Ioánnis. If you look behind during these two kilometers and before you get to the junction to the monastery, you will enjoy a splendid view of the entire Éxo Nisí as far as Chóra, which is like a little white mark at the end of the reddish picture and before the endless blue... It is a real painting!

Ignore the two vertical narrow dirt roads to the left, which lead to two little churches, and you get to a junction where you turn left. After approximately 1 km the road ends at a flat area, where the old monastery of Agios Ioánnis Pródromos stands (see p.72). Below the monastery, in the verdant ravine, there is a small waterfall and a path 1,600 m long leading to a sandy beach that has the same name as the monastery.

To the right of the monastery you can see the ruins of the Byzantine Paliókastro and when you look directly to the sea, you can see Anáfi behind the islets to the west of Astypálaia (Pontikoúsa, Ofidoúsa)! The sunset here is absolutely stunning! Return to the junction where you turned to the monastery and now turn slightly to the left (if you turn slightly to the right, you'll get to the church of Profítis Ilías) and, after another 200 m, turn again to the right. From now on, the road is rather difficult. Along the 3 of the 5.5 km of the route to Pánormos, you can see suc-

Aï-Giánnis

Small beach on the way to Pánormos
*(see the islets of Katsagréli, Pontikoúsa, Ofidoúsa)*

cessive small beaches to the left, which are formed in the recesses of Mount Koúklos on the west shore, and little islets.During the last 2 km turn your head to the right and admire the view of the closed bay of Pánormos from afar. The waters are shallow here but there are usually strong winds despite the fact that the bay is protected by the surrounding hills. A very good choice for swimming is the sandy beach of Valáni, which is situated to the left of the road leading down to Pánormos (about 200 m back) and is protected from the wind. Enjoy the crystal clear blue waters.

The closed bay of Pánormos and the namesake beach

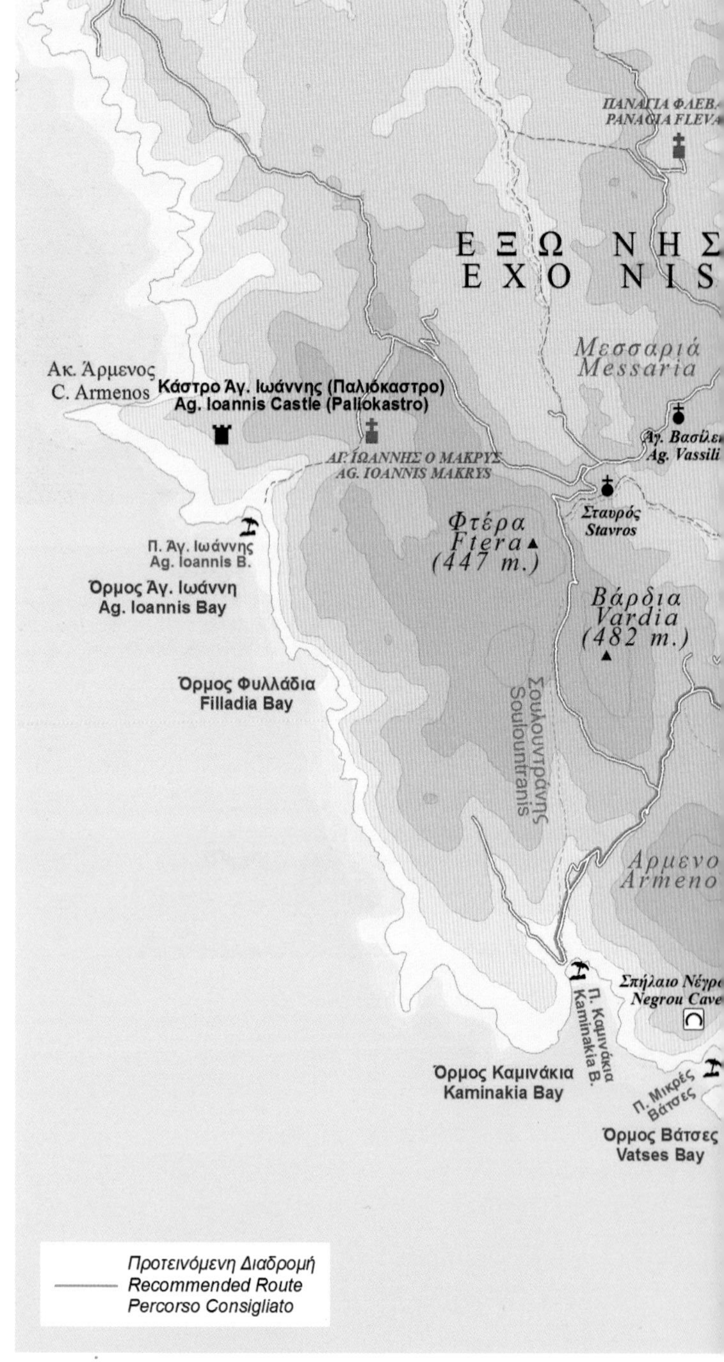
ΠΑΝΑΓΙΑ ΦΛΕΒΑ
PANAGIA FLEVA
ΕΞΩ ΝΗΣ
EXO NIS
Μεσσαριά
Messaria
Ακ. Άρμενος
C. Armenos
Κάστρο Άγ. Ιωάννης (Παλιόκαστρο)
Ag. Ioannis Castle (Paliokastro)
ΑΓ. ΙΩΑΝΝΗΣ Ο ΜΑΚΡΥΣ
AG. IOANNIS MAKRYS
Αγ. Βασίλει
Ag. Vassili
Σταυρός
Stavros
Φτέρα
Ftera
(447 m.)
Π. Άγ. Ιωάννης
Ag. Ioannis B.
Όρμος Άγ. Ιωάννη
Ag. Ioannis Bay
Βάρδια
Vardia
(482 m.)
Όρμος Φυλλάδια
Filladia Bay
Σουλουντράνης
Soulountranis
Αρμενο
Armeno
Σπήλαιο Νέγρ
Negrou Cave
Π. Καμινάκια
Kaminakia B.
Όρμος Καμινάκια
Kaminakia Bay
Π. Μικρές Βάτσες
Όρμος Βάτσες
Vatses Bay
Προτεινόμενη Διαδρομή
Recommended Route
Percorso Consigliato

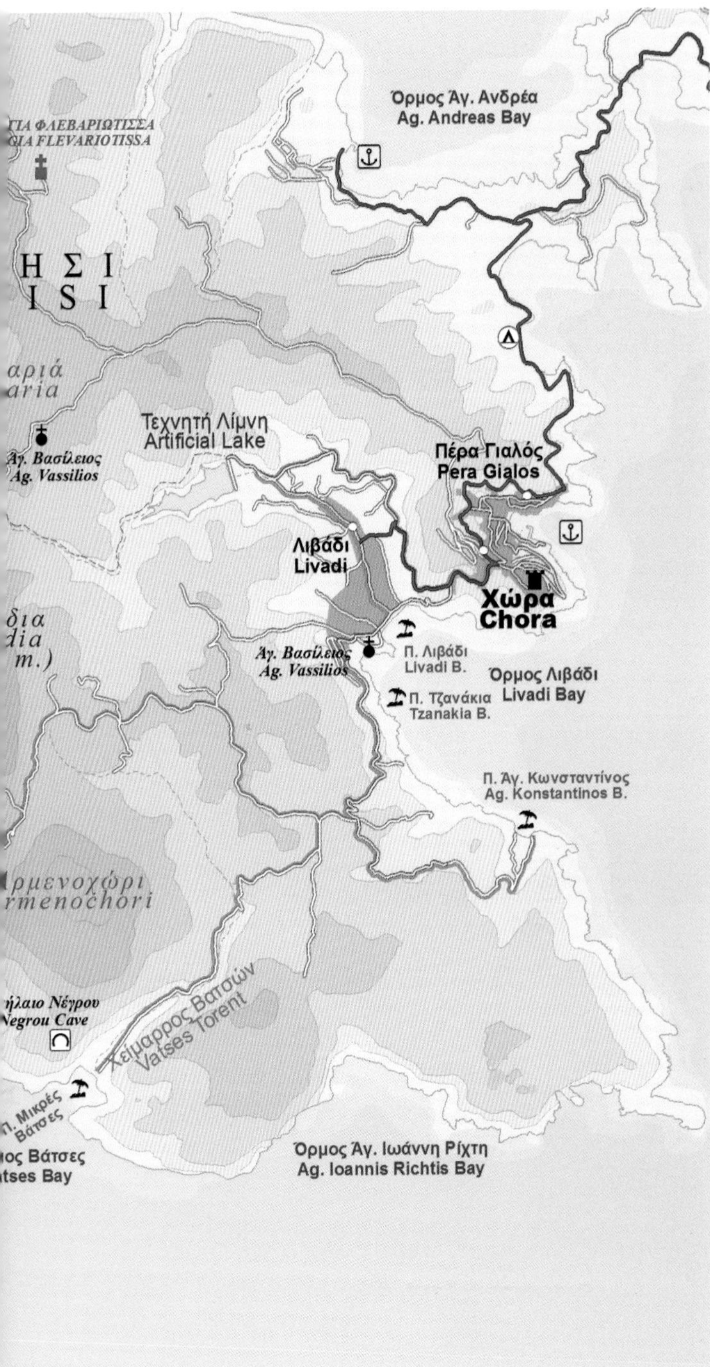
Όρμος Άγ. Ανδρέα
Ag. Andreas Bay
ΓΙΑ ΦΛΕΒΑΡΙΩΤΙΣΣΑ
GIA FLEVARIOTISSA
Η Σ Ι
I S I
Τεχνητή Λίμνη
Artificial Lake
Άγ. Βασίλειος
Ag. Vassilios
Πέρα Γιαλός
Pera Gialos
Λιβάδι
Livadi
Χώρα
Chora
Άγ. Βασίλειος
Ag. Vassilios
Π. Λιβάδι
Livadi B.
Όρμος Λιβάδι
Livadi Bay
Π. Τζανάκια
Tzanakia B.
Π. Άγ. Κωνσταντίνος
Ag. Konstantinos B.
ήλαιο Νέγρου
Negrou Cave
Χείμαρρος Βατσών
Vatses Torent
Π. Μικρές Βάτσες
ος Βάτσες
tses Bay
Όρμος Άγ. Ιωάννη Ρίχτη
Ag. Ioannis Richtis Bay

## South Éxo Nisí

Follow the road from Chóra to Livádi. Do not turn left the downhill road that leads directly to the beach but continue in the direction indicated by the sign Livádi-Frágma (dam). After approximately 3 km you get to the earth dam of the artificial lake of Livádi, which was constructed in 1997. The lake solved to a great extent the water supply problems of Astypálaia since its 1,000,000 m3 that come from the namesake torrent of Livádi cover the irrigation needs of the plain and provide drinking water.

The maximum depth is 25 m and considerable numbers of freshwater fish live in the lake. If, from the road you came, you look down and left, you can see the little church of Sotíros Christoú (Jesus Saviour), where a celebration is held on the day of the Transfiguration, on August 6.

Go the route backwards and reach the junction to Livádi, where you went past some time ago; now turn right. Enter the settlement and, after a few metres, you reach the cement bed of the torrent, which now serves as the main road of the village. You can notice that the snow-white walls of the cottages are quite high. This is because the bed-road you are standing now is sometimes flooded in winter due to the overflowing lake. The road ends at the bridge of the coastal road that comes from the descent of Chóra.

The artificial lake of Livádi

Turn right at "Gefýri" mini market and go west after the coastal road with the shops and the little tables by the water. The organized beach of Livádi is one of the most popular on the island.

Follow the road that runs uphill to the right after the end of the beach and, after a while, you will find a dirt

View of Livádi from the dam

road to the left, which leads to the Early Christian basilica and to the little church of Agios Vassíleios on the hill. Return to the main asphalt road and continue along the coast in a constantly developing area.

Chóra is to the left, while successive beaches open up down below. They all are beautiful: Tzanákia, Mourá, Pápou. Go past the junction you find to the right, which leads to Vátses and Kamınákia, and continue along the asphalt road. It carries on for less than 1 km before it turns into a dirt road exactly at the borders of the area of Archávali, where remarkable finds from the Cycladic period have been discovered. The road leads to the wonderful beach of Agios Konstantínos with the namesake little church on the little hill –to the right as you look at the sea– and the magnificent view of Chóra. It is a very beautiful beach with sand, small pebbles and natural shade from tamarisks.

There are a beach bar and a pretty little tavern. Go back to the junction you went past before and this time turn left. Turn again left at the following junction; do not worry at all, there are informative signs.

After a beautiful 3-km long way along the ravines of Linopótamos and Vátses, you reach the beach of Vátses. It is one of the most famous and popular on the island. A beautiful pebbled beach with a pretty beach bar to the right. Although the beach is directed south, it is afflicted quite often by north winds blowing through the gorge of the namesake ravine that ends there.

The cave of Négrou is situated on the right slope that surrounds the beach (Koutéla), at 150 m above sea level. It was named after a pirate from Sámos called Négros (negro), who,

The small beach of Agios Vassíleios

The beach of Agios Konstantínos

Vátses

according to legend, hid his treasures there. It is a big and beautiful cave with stalagmites and stalactites but, as it happens with the cave of Drákou in Mésa Nisí, it has not been developed and access is rather difficult.

A second smaller cave exists within a short distance. Return to the route of the ravine and at the junction, before the asphalt road, turn left. Continue up the hill of Vouní ignoring all minor dirt roads on both sides that lead to little churches, and reach the plateau of Armenochóri.

As you can see, the area is quite fertile and archaeological excavations have shown that it has continuously been inhabited since Prehistoric years. After you go past the church of Agios Panteleímon to the left (a great religious celebration is held here on July 27), you drive alongside the big

The twin little churches Pétros kai Pávlos (Peter and Paul) on the way to Kaminákia

Kaminákia

Negrou Cave

ravine of the torrent Soulountránis. Approximately 2 km after the pretty twin little churches of Pétros and Pávlos (Peter and Paul), you reach Kaminákia. It is a very beautiful south beach with fine pebbles and natural shade from tamarisks.

One of the most beautiful on the island! There are two taverns before the beach. The second one, the tavern of Línda, is "drowned" in orchards with vegetables, while the garden of the tavern is adorned with a wonderful draw well of 1918!

Anything you find here is produced in the family pen near the mountain of Ftéra and is fished by private fishing boats. Even the bread is kneaded and baked here in the tavern!

The tavern of Linda at Kaminákia with the draw well

# ALTERNATIVE TOURISM

## Climbing

In recent years there have been efforts for the development of this type of tourism, which attracts increasing numbers of tourists to Greece. Most Greek islands, particularly in the Aegean, are recommended for climbing. The same happens with Astypálaia, which is an ideal destination for climbers.

At the top of Ftéra, almost at the centre of Éxo Nisí, the proper climbing equipment, including stainless steel M10 plugs, has been installed on the limestone rock, helping the adventurous climbers with their attempt to climb up the approximately 20 routes of the two areas. The height of the routes ranges from 10 to 90 m and the level of difficulty, according to the French system, is between 4c and 6c.

Access to climbing fields is through a trafficable dirt road, within approximately 20 minutes from Chóra (follow the way to Aï-Giánnis o Makrýs and at the junction at the church of Stavroú turn left alongside the mountain tops.

Ftéra

The overall distance from Chóra is approximately 7.5 km). Apart from Ftéra, new climbing fields are opened on the vertical cliffs above the beach of Vátses, in Aï-Giánnis and in Kókkinos Gremós.

## Mountain biking

The semi-mountainous terrain of the island, with the wide variety of the landscape and the dirt roads in the interior, is ideal for mountain biking. Consult the new ROAD map for the type of route as well as this guide (chapter: Routes of the Island) for the routes you will follow, get your gear and go!

Whichever route you may choose your senses will be rewarded!

## Water Activities

Apart from common water activities and sports (wind surfing, free diving, fishing) you can enjoy in the surrounding waters, the bottom of the sea around the island hides some interesting wrecks. In the area of Floúda Cape (the NE edge of Astypálaia in Mésa Nisí), there are two sunken ships of the German convoy "Olympus," which was attacked in October 1943 by British warships. The second wreck, which is near the neighboring Vourlídia Cape, is in very good condition.

# BEACHES

The sinuous coastline of the island forms dozens of beaches.

Some with fine pebbles, others with sand and some with natural shade, though all of them with crystal clear waters. The most important of them are presented in the following table together with all the information required by a visitor. The beaches are presented clockwise with regard to the map of Astypálaia, starting from the old port of Péra Gialós in Chóra. It is only certain that apart from the beaches of the table, you can discover other minor or private beaches along the coastline (for example, below the hill of the castle, to the south).

In my opinion, the most beautiful beaches of Astypálaia are not on the main island but on the little islets of Kounoúpi and Koutsomýtis.

The exotic beach at the islet of KOUNOUPOI

| NAME | LOCATION | DISTANCE FROM CHORA (km) | ACCESS | ORGANIZED | ORGANIZED | BEACH BAR | NATURAL SHADE | TYPE | COMMENTS |
|---|---|---|---|---|---|---|---|---|---|
| **PERA GIALOS** | In front of the settlement of Péra Gialós | 0,5 | Easy | √ | √ | √ | √ | PEBBLE | View of the castle. Bus stop. |
| **LIVADI** | In front of the settlement of Livadi | 1,2 | Easy | √ | √ | √ | √ | PEBBLE | View of Chóra. Bus stop. |
| **AGIOS VASSILEIOS** | After the small peninsula to the right of Livadi | 1,7 | Downhill path for 100 m | | | | √ | SAND | Bus stop |
| **TZANAKIA** | The first beach on the south coast of the cove of Livadi | 2,1 | Path 300m. | | | | | PEBBLE | Four successive small beaches. View of Chóra. Preferred by nudists. Bus stop. Not visible from the road. |
| **MOURA** | The second beach on the south coast of the cove of Livadi | 2,5 | | | | | | PEBBLE | View of Chóra. |
| **PAPOU** | The third beach on the south coast of the cove of Livadi | 4,3 | | | | | | PEBBLE | View of Chóra. |
| **AGIOS KONSTANTINOS** | Beneath the namesake monastery | 5,5 | Easy | √ | √ | √ | √ | PEBBLE | View of Chóra. Go also by private bus. |
| **LANTES A** | The first beach to the right of Agios Konstantinos | 5,8 | | | | | | PEBBLE | |
| **LANTES B** | The second beach to the right of Agios Konstantinos | 5,9 | | | | | | PEBBLE | |
| **AGIOS IOANNIS RICHTIS** | In the cove forming to the south between the mountains of Echeilí and Athymadári | 8,5 | Path 700 m after the namesake little church | | | | | PEBBLE | |
| **VATSES** | At the estuary of the namesake torrent | 7 | Dirt Road | √ | | √ | √ | PEBBLE | Go also by private bus |

Kaminákia

| NAME | LOCATION | DISTANCE FROM CHORA (km) | ACCESS | ORGANIZED | ORGANIZED | BEACH BAR | NATURAL SHADE | TYPE | COMMENTS |
|---|---|---|---|---|---|---|---|---|---|
| KAMINAKIA | At the estuary of the torrent Soulountranis | 10 | Dirt Road | √ | √ |  | √ | SAND | Go also by private bus |
| AGIOS IOANNIS MAKRYS | Beneath the namesake monastery | 12,7 | Dirt road and 40 min downhill path |  |  |  |  | SAND |  |
| KATSIDONI | SW of Paliokastro | X | Access only by sea |  |  |  |  | SAND |  |
| KLEFTOLIMANO | At the NW edge of the island | 12,7 | Dirt road and 400 m path |  |  |  |  | PEBBLE |  |
| VALANI | The first beach of Panormos from the north | 14,1 | Dirt road and 5 min path |  |  |  |  | PEBBLE |  |
| PANORMOS | In the namesake cove | 14,4 | Dirt Road |  |  |  |  | PEBBLE | Shallow waters |
| PACHEIA AMMOS | The next beach A of Panormos, after the peninsula of Déma | 9,6 | Dirt road and 2.5 hours path after Flevariotissa |  |  |  | √ | SAND |  |
| KAMBANA | At the estuary of the namesake torrent, in the north bay |  | Access only by sea |  |  |  |  | PEBBLE |  |
| VLYCHADA | At the estuary of the torrent Dragounás, in the north bay | X | Access only by sea |  |  |  |  | PEBBLE |  |
| AGIOS ANDREAS | Before the port | 6 | Easy |  |  |  |  | SAND |  |
| CHRYSI AKTI | At the end of the dirt road after the airport | 11,8 | Dirt Road |  |  |  |  | SAND |  |
| PSILI AMMOS | At the north deepest point of the channel before Mésa Nisí | 13,2 | Dirt Road |  |  |  |  | SAND |  |
| MEGALO VAÏ | The first on the west coast of Mésa Nisí | 13,7 | Dirt Road |  |  |  |  | PEBBLE |  |

Vátses

| NAME | LOCATION | DISTANCE FROM CHORA (km) | ACCESS | ORGANIZED | ORGANIZED | BEACH BAR | NATURAL SHADE | TYPE | COMMENTS |
|---|---|---|---|---|---|---|---|---|---|
| MIKRO VAÏ | At the fish farms | 16,3 | Dirt Road | | | | | PEBBLE | |
| ZAFEIRIANI | To the right of the road to Vathý | X | Access only by sea | | | | | PEBBLE | |
| AGIOS FOKAS | At the end of the path from Poularianí to the namesake little church | 21,8 | | | | | | SAND | |
| VRYSI | At the right deepest point of the channel before Mésa Nisí | 13,2 | | | | | | PEBBLE | |
| SCHOINONTAS | In front of the settlement of Schoinóntas | 10,5 | Easy | √ | √ | | | SAND | Bus Stop |
| ANALIPSI | In front of the settlement of Análipsi | 10 | Easy | √ | √ | √ | | SAND | Bus Stop |
| MPLE LIMANAKI | At the edge of the cove of Análipsi | 10 | Easy | | | | | SAND | |
| PLAKES | Just before the airport | 9,6 | Short path for 10' | | | | | PEBBLE & SLATE | Bus Stop |
| STENO | The narrowest point of the channel | 7,1 | Easy | √ | | √ | √ | SAND | Bus Stop |
| MARMARI C | At the junction LIMANI-ANLIPSI | 4,4 | Easy | | | | | SAND | Bus Stop |
| MARMARI B | In front of the campsite | 3,6 | Easy | | | | | SAND | Bus Stop |
| KOUTSOMYTIS | On the namesake islet | X | Access only by sea | | | | | PEBBLE | Emerald waters! Swim along the gut between the islets of Koutsomytis and Tigáni. Shallow waters. |
| NISYROS | On the islet of Kounoúpoi | X | Access only by sea | | | | | SAND & PEBBLE | Exotic beach! A strip of sand connects the islets of Kounoúpoi! Shallow waters. |

The organized beach at Livádi

# LOCAL CUISINE SHOPPING

The original and traditional cuisine of Astypálaia uses mainly products that can be found in abundance on the island, such as fish and seafood, goat meat, saffron and honey.

The extremely delicious cheese, the famous "chlorí," is a typical product of the island. It is a soft type of white cheese that you cannot find anywhere else due to the limited production and the short expiry date (4-5 days). Do not fail to taste "ksialína," the local yogurt. Something that may impress you is the yellow colour you will see in dishes with rice or pasta, or even in buns. It comes from the wild saffron used widely in local cuisine and confectionery. A very famous fish is the roasted fish (mainly salema), which is accompanied with rice and saffron. Restaurant menus include many different dishes of local goat meat cooked in several ways.

Here are some recipes you can only find in Astypálaia.

## Lambrianós

The Easter lamb (or goat) cooked in a different way from the usual followed in the rest of Greece. Apart from Easter, it is also served in several religious celebrations, such as the feast of Portaítissa.

**Ingredients:**

- the body of a medium lamb or goat with its haslets
- 2 kg of rice for soup
- 2 big onions
- pepper, pimentom cinnamon powder,clove-gillyflower
- salted water (almi)
- wax-paper sheets, aluminum foil, needle and thread.

**Execution:** *wash the lamb and put it in the salted water for 1 hour. Wash the haslets and boil them for 5 to 10 minutes. Strain them and cut them in very small pieces. Roast the finely cut onions in a fryer with a little oil, add the finely cut haslets, salt, pepper, pimento (about one teaspoonful), cinnamon and clove-gillyflower (about half a teaspoonful).*

*As soon as the liver is half-ready, add the rice after you have washed it. Finally, add some water, which makes the rice softer. The stuffing is ready and you can remove it from the fire.*

*Take the lamb out of the salted water and stuff it. Stitch carefully the open side of the lamb and sprinkle the spices. Soak the wax-paper sheets into the salted water and wrap the meat. Then you wrap it with the aluminum foil. Place some vines in a roasting pan and put the meat on top. Add some water and roast for 8 hours at a very low temperature.*

## Arantistá

A "scanty" though very delicious dish with pulses.

**Ingredients:**

- 1\2 kg of lentils
- 2 tomatoes
- half a cup of olive oil
- 1 medium onion
- a little tomato paste for colouring
- 2 laurel leaves
- 2 cloves of garlic
- salt
- pepper
- 1\2 kg of water
- 2 cups of flour
- spearmint
- vinegar.

**Execution:***put the lentils, the finely chopped tomatoes and the oil in a cooking pot with water until the lentils are boiled.*

*Pour some oil in a fryer and roast the chopped onion.*

*After you have fried it, put it inside the pot with the lentils. In a bowl mix the flour with the water and knead it until it becomes small balls. Put the balls in the pot with the lentils and add some spearmint and more vinegar.*

### Pouggiá

An exceptional snack with sweet or salted taste

**Ingredients for the dough**
- ½ kg of flour
- 3 spoonfuls of olive oil
- 1 teaspoonful of salt
- 1 egg
- juice of 1 lemon
- some water.

**Ingredients for sweet taste**
- "chlorí" cheese
- cinnamon
- sugar
- milk.

**Ingredients for salted taste**
- kopanistí cheese
- 1 egg
- some water
- spearmint.

**Execution:** *put the ingredients for the dough in a big bowl and knead until it becomes fluffy. Take small lumps of dough and press them to create small pies. Place the stuffing you made on the one side of the pie and fold the other side by pressing the edges. Put the pouggiá in very hot oil and roast them on both sides until they redden. Take them out of the oil and place them on absorbent paper to dry. If you have chosen the sweet stuffing, sprinkle with honey and cinnamon.*

## Shopping

Top quality thyme honey, saffron, oregano, thyme, sage, chamomile, wild mint (pennyroyal), salt from rocks, pasta with saffron, liqueurs from prickly pear, thyme, blueberry and schinus shrubs, the local spoon sweet "élytha" (the male fig) and mandarin sweet, blueberry sweet, lemon flower preserve and pomegranate sweet.

The yellow buns of Astypálaia are famous. They are rusks with saffron and "chlorí" and have a special and spicy taste. You can also buy milk-buns and rusks with oregano.

The local anthótyros ("chlorí") is a must but has a short expiry date. All these local products can be found at the confectionery of Chóra, opposite the town hall, at ILIANNA workshop of traditional products at Provárma, on the road from Chóra to Livádi, and in the mini markets of the island.

Traditional products of Astypálaia

# ACCOMMODATION

On the island there are over 1,500 beds at approximately 100 accommodation spots.

The rooms on the hill of Profítis Ilías and most of those at Péra Gialós offer a wonderful view of Chóra and the castle, while those situated in the old settlement below the castle are more traditional and look at the sea.

The rooms in Livádi and Análipsi are amidst verdant orchards and within a very short distance from the sea.

The price-quality ratio is very good, while almost all of them offer free transportation from the port and the airport.

The campsite of the island is at Marmári and is famous all over the Aegean.

Further below, there is a list of the accommodation spots and the respective information, as in effect at the time when the present guide was published (2016):

# Accomodation at Chora

| OWNER | NAME | TYPE | TELEPHONE NUMBERS (0030) | E-MAIL |
|---|---|---|---|---|
| AGGELIDI AGGELIKI | APHRODITE | STUDIOS | 2243061086-478, 2104200516 6973538235 | info@aphrodite-studios.com |
| AGGELIDI MARIA | VIVA MARE | STUDIOS | 2243061571-572-292 | info@astypaleavivamare.gr |
| VERGOULI STAVROULA | ASTYPALAIA PALACE | HOTEL | 2243061351-925 | astypalaia-palace @hotmail.com |
| VERGOULIS ANTONIS | ONEIRO | STUDIOS | 2243061351-925 | oneiro_apt@hotmail.com |
| GIANNAROU IOANNA | AGERI | STUDIOS | 2243061515-777, 6972876945 6945022618 | ageristudios@hotmail.com |
| GIANNIKAKIS ANTHIMOS | ARCHONTIKO | STUDIOS | 2243061929-760, 6979811551 | info@arhodiko.gr |
| GRIGORIS MICHALIS | ANDROMEDA RESORT | HOTEL | 2243061128-59865, 6979635332 | irini@andromedaresort.gr |
| KALI ANNA | ANATOLI | STUDIOS | 2243061289-680, 6978432442 | gazozas@hotmail.com |
| KAMBOURI FOTINI | FOTINI | HOUSE | 2243061305 | |
| KAMBOURIS ANTONIS | LEFKANTHEMO | STUDIOS | 2243062054, 6974877162 | studios@lefkanthemo.gr |
| KARAMBERI FOTINI | SATINO MARE | STUDIOS | 6944183398 | info@satinomare.gr |
| KAPSI VIRGINIA | ASVESTOTI | STUDIOS | 2243061475, 2104280107 6974351999 | asvestoti@yahoo.gr |
| KOUTSOLIOUTSOS SIMOS | OLTRE MARE | STUDIOS | 210-2020240, 2243061456 | simosk@hol.gr |
| KYRANNOS MICHELIS | KALDERIMI | HOTEL | 2243059843-59844-61120 | info@kalderimi.gr |
| LEMIS IOANNIS | KILINDRA | STUDIOS | 2243061130-131 | studioskilindra@otenet.gr |
| MARIAKIS IOANNIS | MARIAKIS | STUDIOS | 2243061413-62072 | mariakishotel@gmail.com |
| MARIAKIS MICHALIS | THOLARIA | HOTEL | 2243061413-62072 | tholariahotel@gmail.com |
| KALLICHORON PARTNERSHIP | KALLICHORON | STUDIOS | 2243061934, 6937439359 6942801829 | info@kallichoron.gr |
| PALATIANOU EVDOKIA | EVDOKIA'S ROOMS | STUDIOS | 2243061316, 6974358572 2109717521 | evdokiasrooms@gmail.com |
| PAPANIKOLA ARGYRO | PAPANIKOLA | STUDIOS | 6973713996, 2243061014 2104953197 | |
| PETRIDENAS DIMITRIOS | ANEMOMYLOS | STUDIOS | 2243061767, 6946262671 | petridenas@yahoo.gr |
| PETRIDENAS DIMITRIOS | PYLAIA | HOTEL | 2243061001-61070, 6976885922 | info@pylaiahotel.gr |
| PILATOU KALLIOPI | AGNANTI | STUDIOS | 2243061717, 6932224941 | |
| PIPINOU KALLIOPI | POPI | STUDIOS | 2243061404, 6948941684 | kaliopipk@yahoo.gr |
| STAVLAS NIKOLAOS | PROVARMA | STUDIOS | 2243061228-61800 | provarma@yahoo.gr |
| CHRYSOCHOS MICHALIS | ASPRO-MPLE | STUDIOS | 2243061643, 6974610067 | eleni_chris@hotmail.com |

# Accomodation at Analipsi



| OWNER | NAME | TYPE | TELEPHONE NUMBERS (0030) | E-MAIL |
|---|---|---|---|---|
| ALAKIOTI MARIA | AIOLOS | STUDIOS | 2243061563, 6970911040<br>2242020825 | alakiotimaria@hotmail.com |
| ALAKIOTIS MICHAEL | POSEIDON | STUDIOS | 2243061044-842 / 6988467409 | info@poseidon-astypalaia.gr |
| ANASTASIOU - LAPATA | MALTEZANA BEACH | HOTEL | 2243061558, 2107713301 | info@maltezanabeach.gr |
| GRIGORI EFIMIA | PANORAMA | STUDIOS | 2243061347-747, 6976827047 | info@panoramastudios.gr |
| DELMADOROU ANAST. | AGNANTI | STUDIOS | 2243061102-466, 6977186671 | info@agnadi-astypalaia.gr |
| DELMADOROU ELENI | 7 STARS | STUDIOS | 2243061957, 2105613268<br>6972450282 | info@7asteria.gr |
| ZIOVA MARIA | CASTELLANO | HOTEL | 2243064010, 6942075075<br>6938536095 | info@castellanovillage.gr |
| KALI DIANA | DIANA | STUDIOS | 2243061204, 6973576844 | kaligianna@gmail.com<br>diana@astypalaia.info |
| KALI IRINI | MALTEZANA | STUDIOS | 2243061446-203 | |
| KALIS ILIAS | MALTEZANA | STUDIOS | 2243061446-203 | |
| KRASSA VARVARA | SUNSHINE RESORT | STUDIOS | 2243061502, 2105625514<br>6980261757 | sunshine@astypalaia.info |
| KOSTOPOULOU AGGELINA | AKROTIRI | STUDIOS | 2243061586, 6976792268<br>2105614352, 6948509223 | tkontaratos@yahoo.gr |
| MAKRIS ROUSSETOS | OASIS | STUDIOS | 2243061115, 6976539726 | kostasmakris2@hotmail.com |
| PATINIOTI ZAMBELOU | OVELIX | STUDIOS | 2243061260, 6985737154 | |
| PATINIOTIS KONSTANTINOS | CASTILLIO | HOTEL | 2243061552-553, 6977258673-4<br>2104943287 | hotel@castillio.gr |
| POLOU VARVARA | VILLA BARBARA | STUDIOS | 2243061448, 6930778530<br>6946329605 | |
| SKARTADOU MARIA | MELTEMI | STUDIOS | 2243061094, 6946353460 | |
| SMYRNIOU EFTHYMIA | RODIA | STUDIOS | 2243061622-610, 6972314946<br>6932375994 | smirnios@otenet.gr<br>rodiastudios@hotmail.com |

# Accomodation at Livadi

| OWNER | NAME | TYPE | TELEPHONE NUMBERS (0030) | E-MAIL |
|---|---|---|---|---|
| AGGELIDI VIRGINIA | ASTRA | STUDIOS | 2243061381-270, 6974174627 | astrastudios@gmail.com |
| AGGELIDIS ANTONIOS | MAGANAS | HOTEL | 2243061468, 6976657853 | info@maganashotel.gr |
| VENETOS DIMITRIOS | VENETOS | STUDIOS | 2243061490 | venetospelagia.astypalaia @gmail.com |
| GEORGOSTATHIS ILIAS | FILDISI | HOTEL | 2243062060, 6978445434 | info@fildisi.net |
| GIANNARAKIS PETROS | KARAVO | HOTEL | 2243061782-783 | info@hotelkarabo.gr |
| GIANNAROS MICHAEL | KALOUDIS | STUDIOS | 2243061318, 6971873436 | pansion-kaloudis@hotmail.gr |
| GIANNAROS MICHAEL | GERANI | STUDIOS | 2243061484-337, 6942263926 | info@astypalaiagerani.gr |
| GIANNAROS PETROS | LILOS | STUDIOS | 2243061034 | liselotte.giannarou@gmx.de |
| GIANNAROU GEORGIA | GEORGIA | STUDIOS | 2243061018-017-580, 6944350394 | |
| GIANNAROU IRINI | IRINI | STUDIOS | 2243061318, 6971873436 | pansion-kaloudis@hotmail.gr |
| DROUGA MARIA | DROUGAS | STUDIOS | 2243061150, 6944301381 | info@astypalaiastudios.gr |
| KALI-RAPTI KALLIOPI | ASTERIAS | STUDIOS | 2243061298, 2104535219 6937758580 | kallipopi@hotmail.com |
| KARAGEORGIOU GEORG. | ESPERIS | STUDIOS | 2243061230-458, 6942674496 | esperis_studios@yahoo.gr |
| KARAGEORGIOU MARIA | ESPERIS | STUDIOS | 2243061230-458, 6942674496 | esperis_studios@yahoo.gr |
| KOKKINOU AGGELIKI | ASTYPALAIA VILLAS | STUDIOS | 2243062015, 2106526490 6948401473 | ag_kokkinou@yahoo.com |
| KOMINEAS NIKOLAOS | ARCHITEKTONIKI | HOTEL | 2243061339-59830-59831 | nkomin@tee.gr info@arhitektoniki.gr |
| KONTARATOU MARIA | ANIXI | STUDIOS | 2243061269 | anixistudios@hotmail.com |
| MANOLAKI MARIA | SALONIKIA | STUDIOS | 6948301980, 2104283306 work 2104119923 home | salonikiastudios@yahoo.com |
| MARIAKI MARIA | MPAKSES | STUDIOS | 2243061582, 6979930514 | o_mpakses@hotmail.com |
| PALATIANOU EVDOKIA | EVDOKIA'S ROOMS | STUDIOS | 2243061316, 6974358572 2109717521 | evdokiasrooms@gmail.com |
| TEZARI AGGELIKI | MOURAS RESORT | RESIDENCE | 2243061127-227, 6972453571 | info@mourasresort.gr reception@mourasresort.gr |
| TEZARI-GIANNARAKI AGGELIKI | MOURAS | STUDIOS | 2243061127-227 / 6972453571 | info@mourastudios.gr |
| HATZIBYROU MARIA | FILOXENIA | STUDIOS | 2243061650-656, 6946190776 2104526311 | linahatzi@hotmail.com |

# Accomodation at Pera Gialos

| OWNER | NAME | TYPE | TELEPHONE NUMBERS (0030) | E-MAIL |
|---|---|---|---|---|
| AGGELIDI VIRGINIA | VIVA MARE | STUDIOS | 2243061571-572-292 | ja@astypaleatours.gr |
| AGGELIDIS FRANGISKOS | PARADISSOS | HOTEL | 2243061224 | hotelparadissos@hotmail.com |
| ACHLADIOTI AIKATERINI | KAITI | STUDIOS | 2243061375 | marina_axladioti@hotmail.com |
| ACHLADIOTI KALI | POPI | STUDIOS | 2243061267 | helenakladioti608@hotmail.com |
| VAOLA IRINI (2) | ADELAODA | STUDIOS | 2243061171 | |
| VENETOS IOANNIS | VENETOS | STUDIOS | 2243061643/6972941846 | nikivenetou@hotmail.com |
| GEORGIADIS STEFANOS | ANEMOSYRIS | STUDIOS | 2243061555 | stemar3@otenet.gr |
| GIANNAROU MARIA | ORSALIA | STUDIOS | 2243061559-983, 6976200597 | kostantinos_gian@hotmail.com |
| KAMBOURI EVANGGELIA | DELFINI | STUDIOS | 2243061716 - 61863 | kabpav@yahoo.com |
| LAPATA MARIA | ANGELA | STUDIOS | 2243061343-561, 6979296055 2103233373 | |
| MANOLAKI MARIA | PSAROS | STUDIOS | 2243061127, 6972453571 | manmar_70@yahoo.gr psarosstudios@yahoo.gr |
| MINAS STELIOS | THALASSA | HOTEL | 2243059840 | info@stampalia.gr |
| MOURIDOU ZAMBELLOU | BELLI | STUDIOS | 2243061028, 2105443043 6973885569 | studiosbelli@gmail.com |
| NIKOLAKI-VOGIATZI MARGARITA | XENIOS DIAS | STUDIOS | 2243061247-074 | xeniosdias@astypalaia.info |
| EKONOMOU MARIA-IRINI | ASTYNEA | HOTEL | 2243061040-355, 6946738337 | astyneahotel@yahoo.gr |
| PAPANIKOLA ARGYRO | PAPANIKOLA | STUDIOS | 6973713996, 2243061014 2104953197 | |
| PATINIOTI IRINI | CALDERA | STUDIOS | 2243061083, 6978892601 | astypal@otenet.gr |
| PATINIOTI MARGARITA | KARLOS | STUDIOS | 2243061330, 6982211850 | karlos_rooms@hotmail.com |
| PETRIDENA ASIMINA | AKTI | STUDIOS | 2243061001-070-114 6976885922 | info@aktirooms.gr |
| PODOTA EFROSYNI | STAMPALIA | STUDIOS | 2243061200, 6974753665 | stampalia65@yahoo.gr |
| SKARTADOU EFROSYNI | AVRA | STUDIOS | 2243061363, 6937372124 | skartados@gmail.com |
| STAVLA DIMITRA | AQUA BLUE | STUDIOS | 2243061067 | |
| STAVLA MARIA | AUSTRALIA | STUDIOS | 2243061855 | pmariaki@hotmail.com |
| STAVLAS THEODOROS | VYTHOS | STUDIOS | 2243061880, 6972089561 | aggeliki.trip@gmail.com |
| HARALAMBI-KONTARATOU EFROSYNI | MAOSTRALI | STUDIOS | 2243061233-691, 6945377944 | frou28@hotmail.com |
| HARALAMBI-KONTARATOU EFROSYNI | ICHTHYΣESSA | HOTEL | 2243061233-691, 6945377944 | frou28@hotmail.com |
| HATZIDAKI ELENI | KORALI | STUDIOS | 2243061808-462, 6972096937 | astypalaiakorali@hotmail.com |
| HATZIDAKI ELENI | VOTSALO | HOTEL | 2243061808-462, 6972096937 | info@votsalostudios.gr |

# FOOD

Pretty tavern at Péra Gialós

In the little taverns of Astypálaia you can find the original Aegean cuisine. There are no brand names here but only little family fish taverns and restaurants.

Although the food in Astypálaia is everywhere delicious and quite cheap, here are some of these places. In Péra Gialós, you can eat at the traditional tavern of Akrogiáli.

The tables are on the sand and the spot offers a wonderful view of the castle. In my opinion, this is the best choice! In Chóra, try Ágoni Grammí on the square with the windmills, while for more gourmet tastes you should visit the restaurant Barbarossa next to the town hall.

In Livádi a very good choice is Geráni, while in Maltezána the seaside tavern of Astyfagiá and Análipsi in Schoinóntas.

You can also find very good food at Linda's restaurant in Kaminákia and in the little tavern on the beach of Agios Konstantínos.

Panoramic view of Chóra

**ALL CAFES, RESTAURANTS & ACCOMMODATION SPOTS, OFFER Wi-Fi CONNECTION TO VISITORS!**

# ENTERTAINMENT

The island offers choices for every taste, starting from pretty bars and cafes in the three settlements of the islands to say the least! In the quarter of Megáli Panagía of Chóra, under the magnificent castle walls, you can find the namesake bar-cafe Castro (castle) with the fantastic view of the sea. It serves wonderful cocktails and organizes live music events. At Artemis bar, in the quarter of Pálos, there is jazz, reggae and rock music throughout the year, while you may also watch live events with beautiful Greek songs or stand-up comedy performances. A few metres from the windmills you can find the pretty bar Mýlos. Splendid view with atmospheric music and cool cocktails in the bar-cafes of Archipélagos and Théa of Chóra. If you prefer Greek music, then the clubs Koúros and Panórama are just for you. At the centre, beside and behind the town hall, you can find the beautiful cafe Nótos and the traditional cafe tou Mouggoú. Finally, do not miss the cafe Meltémi with its delicious homemade sweets at the central square!

Walk out of Chóra and follow the road down to Péra Gialós. Along the coast you can find the cafes En Plo, La Luna, Dápia, with a wonderful view of the old port and the castle, the cafe Parádeisos (ask for cold yogurt sweet!), while at the junction between Péra Gialós and the ring road of Chóra do not miss the club La Punta with good Greek music. Very beautiful is also the traditional cafe-snack Argó on the uphill part of the road from Gialós to Chóra, which organizes several live music events with traditional, rembétika and modern Greek songs.

If you want something minimal, then the cafe-bar Allegro on the coast

The magnificent traditional cafes in Maltezána

of Livádi is the place to be, while very close to it you can enjoy yourselves at the cafe-bar Royal, which attracts young people. For more advanced choices, do not miss the lunch cafe-bar Mojito.

It has already been reported that Análipsi offers the beautiful traditional cafes of Maltézos and Marínos.

Outside the settlements you can find the club Mamounia, at the bend before the junction leading to the port of Agios Andréas, which offers food, drinks and many live events. Do not forget the little bar of the campsite at Marmári, with the famous rembétika nights! If you want something cozier and friendlier but not necessarily a hangout, then there will always be some guys with their guitars singing and having fun under the windmills in the sweet summer nights...

# USEFUL TELEPHONE NUMBERS

| | PLACE | TEL.(0030) |
|---|---|---|
| TOWN HALL | CHORA | 2243061206 |
| MUNICIPAL TOURIST AGENCY | CHORA *(INSIDE A WINDMILL)* | 2243061412 |
| POLICE | PERA GIALOS | 2243060207 |
| PORT AUTHORITIES | PERA GIALOS | 2243061208 |
| CUSTOMS | PERA GIALOS | 2243061317 |
| SURGERY | RING ROAD | 2243061222 |
| PHARMACY | CHORA-PERA GIALOS ROAD | 2243061444 |
| SOCIETY OF VOLUNTEERS FOR THE CIVIL PROTECTION | CHORA | 2243061999 |
| AIRPORT | ANALIPSI | 2243061410 |
| OLYMPIC - AEGEAN | PERA GIALOS | 2243061665 |
| BLUE STAR AGENCY | PERA GIALOS | 2243061224 |
| ANEK KALYMNOS AGENCY | PERA GIALOS | 2243061665<br>2243061571 |
| TOURIST AGENCY | PERA GIALOS | 2243062130 |
| POST OFFICE | CHORA | 2243061223 |
| ACS COURIER | RING ROAD | 2243059888 |
| SPEEDEX COURIER | CHORA-PERA GIALOS ROAD | 2243061444 |
| GENIKI TACHYDROMIKI COURIER | RING ROAD | 2243061913 |
| ALPHA BANK | PERA GIALOS | 2243059893 |
| NATIONAL BANK (AGENT) | PERA GIALOS | 2243061224 |
| ASSOCIATION OF RENTAL ROOMS | PERA GIALOS | 2243061778 |
| ELIN PETROL STATION | CHORA-PERA GIALOS ROAD | 2243061087 |
| ARGO PETROL STATION | MARMARI | 2243061289 |
| CARSHOP | PERA GIALOS | 2243061730 |
| TAXI 1 (GIORGOS-PANTELIS) | CHORA | 6976256461 |
| TAXI 2 (KIKI KALI) | CHORA | 6975706365 |
| GIANNARAKIS TRANSPORT | MARMARI | 2243059848 |
| CULTURAL ASSOCIATION | PERA GIALOS | 2243061566<br>6944384227 |

# AFTERWORD

Astypalaia is so beautiful and fascinating that I really struggled to find a way to finish the book. Therefore, instead of a few words as an afterword, I chose a marvelous tale from the rich folklore tradition of the island...

**"The doll"**

Once upon a time there was a very poor woman who had a daughter. They lived opposite the palace, in the castle. All the time the woman was trying to find a way to escape their poverty and get her daughter a good boy to marry. One day, when she learnt that the prince was leaving for the war, she had an idea and told her daughter:

- Do you know what I have thought? Now that the prince has gone to war, I should go to the queen and tell her that one day that I was away to bring water, the prince found the door open, came in, abused you, and now you are pregnant with his child.

- Mother, what are talking about? I don't know the prince; we have never exchanged a word!

- I am going to the palace and you keep your thoughts for yourself. We are desperate and the queen will believe me and provide for our food. For her grandchild!

Despite the cries and the shouts of the girl, the woman did not change her mind and set off for the palace. The servants asked the queen for her permission and then the woman was presented with the queen:

- Your Highness, I should never cause any inconvenience to you but you must know what has happened!

- This is unbelievable...

- I'm telling you again that I wouldn't be here but my daughter is unable to work and I am very poor to make ends meet and support three people!

- Since my son is responsible, you don't have to worry. I will take care of you and support you.

The woman returned delighted and told her daughter what had happened.

- Mother, do you understand what you have done? When the prince returns, he will definitely kill us! There is no child to show them!

- Let's see if he returns first and then we'll find a way...

The time went by and the woman put some clothes and cushions on her daughter's belly so that she looked pregnant. The queen's servants sent her provisions and everything seemed to be fine. Nine months had passed and the child had to be born! The woman gets a doll, wraps it with diapers and shows it to her daughter:

- Here's your son! I'm going to the palace to tell them the news.

The cunning woman goes to the palace and announces the news to the queen.

- Your Highness, you have a beautiful and healthy grandson! But you cannot come and see him unless forty days have passed, according to the custom.

- Never mind, I can wait a little longer, the queen answered.

In this way the woman earned some more time as well as provisions and gifts for the "newborn baby"... Forty days passed and the time came for the presentation of the baby! The young girl was in panic and was crying all the time but the woman was very calm. She dressed the doll, took her in her hands and set off for the palace. As she was walking up the stairs, where the queen was waiting to see her grandson at last, the woman deliberately stumbled. The doll dropped from her hands and plummeted off the cliff into the sea!

- Oh, what a disaster! the queen cried. Her cries and sobs spread over the entire Chóra.

The crafty woman was afraid of the rage and sadness of the queen and disappeared. The queen felt very sorry for the daughter, whom the woman had taken with her to the palace, and took her inside. Suddenly the fleet of the prince appeared on the horizon! This should be a moment of joy and celebration instead of bereavement and cries because the only son of the queen was coming back alive and victorious. They reveled until late at night, when the prince turned and told his mother:

- Mother, I feel very tired and I am going to bed.

- My son, before you leave I would like to talk to you about something, now that our guests have gone.

The queen recounted the whole story, as she knew it, to the stunned prince.

- I think that you have to marry the girl, my son, the queen said.

- Where is she now, mother? The prince asked.

- She is locked in your bedroom and she is crying for the baby the poor girl lost...

- All-right, mother. Let us alone now, please. We'll meet in the morning.

The prince opened the door and found the girl blubbing uncontrollably. She was so beautiful!

- Can you tell me what is my mother talking about?

- My prince, it's not my fault. Everything was planned by my mother. I know she is so frivolous, but she is not bad. She did it because we were very hungry and poor! But we made a fool of you, I admit it.

She knelt in front of him and bent her neck so that he could take her life. The prince was impressed with the girl's honesty.

- You know what? he told her. One day I was fighting and was in real danger but finally my life was saved. While I was sleeping at night, I had a dream. I saw the Virgin telling me, *"Prince, I saved your life because back in your island there's a beautiful, honest and sensitive girl waiting for you. You have to act like a man!"*

After a few days the prince got married with the beautiful girl and they lived happily ever after!

# BIBLIOGRAPHY REFERENCES


- A. Theodosópoulos: ANEXERÉVNITI ASTYPÁLAIA, ROAD 2005
- L. Xánthos: ASTYPÁLAIA, ISTORÍA KAI ISTORÍES, 2009
- AKOLOUTHÍA OSÍOU ÁNTHIMOU, PORTAÍTISSA MONASTERY, 1911
- MIÁ PETALOÚDA STI MÉSI TOU AIGAÍOU, MUNICIPALITY OF ASTYPÁLAIA, 2014
- M. Kóllia: ARCHEOLOGIKÓ MOUSEÍO ASTYPÁLAIAS MINISTRY OF CULTURE, 1998
- A. Tarsoúli: ASTYPÁLAIA, SÝLLOGOS FÍLON ASTYPÁLAIAS – AGRA PUBLICATIONS, 1996
- S. Leontáris: ÉREVNA EPÍ TIS GEOMORFOLOGÍAS TIS NÍSOU ASTYPÁLAIAS, 1974
- A. Krantonéli: ISTORÍA TIS PEIRATEÍAS, 1390 - 1538, ESTIA PUBLICATIONS, 1998
- DODECANESIAN CHRONICLES, HOUSE OF LETTERS AND FINE ARTS OF THE DODECANESE, YEARLY PUBLICATIONS
- ASTYPÁLAIA: OPERATIONAL DEVELOPMENT PLAN 2014-2020, PREFECTURE OF SOUTH AEGEAN, 2014
- GENERAL CENSUS, HELLENIC STATISTICAL AUTHORITY, 2011
- W. Miller: I FRAGGOKRATÍA STIN ELLÁDA, ELLINIKA GRAMMATA, 1990
- https://astypalaia.wordpress.com
- www.astypalaia.gr
- www.astypalea.net